Farming Grace

A Memoir of Life, Love, and a Harvest of Faith

PAULA SCOTT

FARMING GRACE
by Paula Scott
www.paulascott.com

This book or parts thereof may not be reproduced in any form, stored in a retrieval system, or transmitted in any form by any means—electronic, mechanical, photocopy, recording, or otherwise—without prior written permission of the publisher, except as provided by United States of America copyright law. The names and appearances of some individuals in this story have been changed, and in a few instances, settings have been modified to preserve anonymity.

Cover Design: Jenny Quinlan, historicaleditorial.com
Editors: Kimberly Shumate, Susanne Lakin, Alice Crider, Janet McHenry, and Judy Gordon Morrow
Published in the United States by West Butte Publishing.

Copyright 2019 by Paula Scott Bicknell
All rights reserved

ISBN-10: 0-578-43749-X
ISBN-13: 978-0-578-43749-1

Table of Contents

Prologue 5

Chapter One 15

Chapter Two 21

Chapter Three 31

Chapter Four 41

Chapter Five 51

Chapter Six 59

Chapter Seven 65

Chapter Eight 75

Chapter Nine 87

Chapter Ten 91

Chapter Eleven 101

Chapter Twelve 111

Chapter Thirteen 119

Chapter Fourteen 129

Chapter Fifteen 135

Chapter Sixteen 143

Chapter Seventeen 151

Chapter Eighteen 159

Chapter Nineteen 165

Chapter Twenty 177

Chapter Twenty-One 183

Chapter Twenty-Two 193

Chapter Twenty-Three 201

Chapter Twenty-Four 213

Chapter Twenty-Five 221

Chapter Twenty-Six 229

Chapter Twenty-Seven 233

Epilogue 243

Acknowledgments 251

Prologue

> The most beautiful stories always start with wreckage.
>
> — Jack London

The doctor said I had a breakdown due to physical exhaustion.

"You've had seven kids, four in the last eight years. Your body is drained, dangerously depleted of potassium. Your brain shut off to save your life." This, from a kind, smiling young physician.

"But it doesn't feel physical. It feels spiritual and emotional," I told the doctor.

"I'm sure it does, but your real problem is physical. You need rest and nourishing food. Let's get you started on some vitamins. And can you hire help for around the house? Your large family must be a lot of work for you."

Tears rolled down my cheeks as I laughed at the earnest young physician. Hired help wasn't in my world, and I didn't want to talk about things I couldn't afford. I could hardly afford this medical care. Three days of not knowing who I was, being rushed to the hospital in an ambulance, handcuffed because the sheriffs who came to our house thought I was having a psychotic episode due to drugs.

"Maybe someone slipped her something at that writing conference," one of the fire department paramedics suggested to my husband.

"It was a Christian conference," my husband assured him.

The paramedic raised his eyebrows, as if my husband didn't know poop from a pretzel. "Well, she'll be tested for narcotics at the hospital. It sure looks like drugs to us."

My husband told me the sheriff, who handcuffed me before they stuck me in the ambulance, was overweight. "He had a bald head and big round belly," said my husband.

"Did I cuss him out too?" I asked. It wouldn't have surprised me. I swore at everybody else. Out-of-my-mind cussing coming from a woman who hadn't let a profane word slip past her lips since she gave her life to Christ twelve years earlier. A church lady who carried her Bible everywhere she went and came down hard on her teenagers for saying "holy cow" and "that sucks."

"No, but you called the sheriff 'Santa Claus.' I think you really hurt his feelings."

I wish I could have explained to that poor sheriff that every Christmas Eve the big red fire trucks drove down our dirt road with Santa on board. They came to distribute gifts to all the children in our rural neighborhood. It was a delightful tradition; our family always ran out to meet the trucks, our children dancing with expectation. These weren't cheap, frilly gifts. One year our boys got scooters.

All the farmers and ranchers donated to the cause, so all the country kids got something really nice. I made cookies for the fire crew and handed them out as Santa passed out his parcels. I'm sure when I saw those fire trucks coming, I thought Santa was about to show up.

I wanted to say, "Sheriff Lloyd, it's not your belly or your bald head. I'm just messed up right now and looking for Saint Nick 'cause I'm used to seeing Santa on big red trucks with ladders."

En route to the emergency room, the paramedics freed my hands, replacing the cuffs with cloth restraints—not that I remember it. I vaguely remember hitting my dad in the yard before the police showed up. Slapping him as hard as I could across the face as he tried to calm me down. I was wearing my favorite jeans with holes in the knees. They were Italian jeans that felt like butter against my skin. I'd gotten them at a thrift store in Monterey where rich women dumped their clothes. I'd paid $48 bucks for them. They probably cost $480 brand new. You can buy a fat hog with that kind of money.

After hitting my dad, I grabbed the holes and ripped the jeans off my body. This was probably when my husband and my friend Kay decided it was time to call for help.

I told Kay at the hospital that a deeply buried anger at men drove me over the edge. And maybe in some painfully honest part of my mind, I was angry at God too, but I didn't admit that to Kay or even myself. I was good at burying my feelings. I'd been digging that deep, dark hole for a long time. Stuff it all down. Don't look at it. Don't talk to it. Don't touch it. Put on a sweet smile and plow through life like everything's okay. But everything wasn't okay. When I was coming apart, I told my husband I was a baby donkey. Jesus rode into Jerusalem on a young donkey. Palm Sunday had just passed. The pastor preached about this donkey colt at church a few days earlier. Jesus didn't ride a war horse into town like a conquering king. He came as a humble servant riding a beast of burden, said the pastor. My husband has a literal translation of the Bible. Donkeys are called asses in this translation. Maybe this donkey story got stuck in my head. Or maybe I felt like a beast of burden myself. Women bear such a heavy load these days. Life becomes overwhelming. And extreme. Like a sport that can kill you. Like climbing Mount Everest.

"You gotta be tough," my dad always said. So, I was tough until the day I wasn't anymore. Until my ass went wild and broke free from its yoke in our front yard. When you're tearing off your Italian jeans, out of your mind crazy, people take notice.

But before going crazy, before the handcuffs, the ambulance, and the hospital, I had read a story of a starving little fox that found her way to a good man's farm. Hungry, but scared to death, she refused to take the egg the good man left for her each day. After watching the man for some time, the little fox finally began to taste the egg he offered. At first, she would only take the egg out in the field after the man walked away, but day by day, the man drew her closer and closer to his house until, in great trust, she finally accepted the egg from his hand.

I grew up on a farm and knew about foxes: they're egg thieves. Chicken eaters. Life stealers. Much like the way I lived as a young adult, prowling the edges of grace, thieving it the way we all do before we finally accept it from God's hand. But during those years, I longed to go home, to return to God and to the farm. A starving little fox so hungry for grace.

In 2005, we moved to our farm. My husband had become a high school history teacher after fifteen years in the Army. Our daughters, Cami and Lacy, were in the sixth and fourth grades, our oldest son, Luke, in first grade. John and Joseph were busy toddlers. Along with mothering our brood of five, I was determined to become an author, not a farmer. But the California land in my blood called my name—had been calling me home since I'd left decades earlier for Reno, Nevada, where I'd gone to college.

After following my military man across a continent or two, it felt good to finally settle down and begin our life back home on a quiet country road near the Sacramento River where fruit and nuts grow in abundance. My parents, who lived nearby in the Sutter Buttes—the smallest mountain range in the world—had almonds, but we didn't want to farm those. My brother Patrick, who owned the land beside us, was set on putting in walnuts and stone fruit—primarily peaches, as our grandparents had grown.

Once we cleared off the old almond trees in our front pasture, we put our horses out there to graze. We'd just moved into the house we built, and our living room windows looked over this beautiful field. Several weeks before Easter, a little red fox moved into the pasture with the horses. Early each morning while I sat and read my Bible, I watched her make her rounds, drinking out of the water tank and hunting squirrels under several old almond trees we'd left for shade for the horses. The fox appeared undernourished, and I remembered the fox story of the good man feeding his fox the eggs. So, after our annual Easter egg hunt that year, I gathered up all the leftover hard-boiled eggs, and every day I dropped several near her den—a large hole in the ground.

Pretty soon she grew used to me, and instead of running away when I stepped onto our porch, she waited under the almond tree near her hole, watching me.

In the beginning, she wouldn't touch the Easter eggs, but slowly they became her daily meal. At dawn one day as I was boiling eggs, about a month into this, I watched her carry what I thought was a cottontail to her den. *Good for my little fox*, I decided. *She's feeding herself now. I won't have to keep making her eggs.* Though, I'd gotten quite attached to caring for her.

Within a half an hour, I noticed her crossing the field again with another little rabbit in her mouth. Savoring my coffee, I stared out the window at the little fox's comings and goings.

Watch her closely, the Lord whispered to my heart. Again, she trotted through the grass to a distant place and returned in a short while with another furry ball between her teeth. The sun had now risen above the hills beyond our pasture, turning the sky pink, washing light and warmth over the dew-covered grass. To my utter astonishment, when she came out of the hole, trailing her were four little kits tumbling over each other.

What I had thought were bunnies were really baby foxes!

She trusts you now, and she's proving that trust by bringing her little ones under your care, the Lord said. *Just as you are learning to trust me. Learning that trust comes with time, and the hand of grace that feeds you is tender.*

You see, I was about to undergo a tumultuous passage. My past would have to be plowed before my future could be planted. Above all, I would need to trust the Ultimate Farmer: God. Trust being the first step of every journey.

I come from a long line of strong women with men issues. My great-grandma Delcie Mae, whom the family called Dell, walked to California beside a covered wagon because of a no-good man. When Dell's daddy died, her granddaddy ran off with all the family's money, disappearing down to Texas for no good reason. Dell's grandma and momma went to Texas looking for him but never found the granddaddy.

Thus, two women determined to start over in California set out in a covered wagon full of little girls. Delcie had one older brother and a handful of younger sisters. The twelve-year-old brother walked beside Dell to California. The baby sisters rode in the wagon. One sister died on the journey after her nightgown caught flame in the campfire, and she ran. By the time they wrestled her to the ground, she was badly burned and slipped away a few days later. I hold this against Granddaddy No-good and don't like that his blood runs through my veins.

But Dell's momma Elizabeth—her blood runs through my veins too. She became Granny Phillips when she was old and would fish on the Sacramento River with her grandsons, shaking her fist at any man who dared to move in on her fishing hole. They called it the "Glory Hole," and Elizabeth Granny Phillips wasn't about to share her glory with a no-good man.

"She was a fierce little woman, a hundred pounds soaking wet," the keeper of family secrets once told me. "Men didn't mess with Granny Phillips and her grandsons on the river."

And right then, I dreamed of becoming Elizabeth Granny Phillips, fishing with my grandsons on the river someday, and shaking my fist at men without shame, without fear. Training up my boys and standing up to men who would run a woman off the river.

I absolutely adore the Sacramento River. It begins at a pretty little spring in Mount Shasta, a sleeping volcano, where I've filled a jug full of crystal-clear, ice-cold water coming out of the mountain and drunk it with my kiddos there at the headwaters of the Sacramento. The river runs down into the valley, twisting and turning, a swath of life wherever it flows. The Sacramento reminds me of a wise old woman who has learned to wear something down. Patience is a virtue that will serve you well. Elizabeth knew this. You just outlast people. She outlasted that no-good husband and the men on the river too.

At nineteen years old, I hadn't outlasted anything yet, but I'd already learned the hands of men weren't tender and couldn't be trusted either. I'd arrived in Reno, Nevada, on the tail of a painful breakup with my first honest-to-goodness boyfriend. I call him that because not only did I give him my heart, but also gave him my virginity, which seemed like all of me. Then, he dumped me and slept with other girls. I was devastated. But we got back together—after a month of his sowing his wild oats and a month of me sowing my wild tears—and tried again because I loved him so much. Still, our relationship didn't last.

Just a few months after one turbulent year together, I was on my way to Reno alone, trying to outrun a broken heart. The Biggest Little City in the World—that's what the sign says as you enter the strip of casinos that never close in the shadow of the Sierra Nevada.

And that's where I'd do my first line of cocaine.

Chapter One

> You are not required to set yourself on
> fire to keep other people warm.
>
> — Unknown

Rain fell sideways. A cold wind blew against my face. The newborn calf out in the pasture was sick. Dad picked up the little black baby and carried it to the barn. The momma bawled in protest but didn't charge. She followed at a fast walk, wagging her head back and forth like an angry bull, but I knew she wasn't mad, just upset about her calf. If she were mad, she would have come after us as Dad's mean old bull did. Instead, she followed like a loyal dog. The whole herd trailed behind her through the storm to the barn.

I walked close to Dad as he said over the wind, "If that momma decides to run us down, you race as fast as you can in a zigzag line. I know you're quick. If you don't run straight, she won't catch you. I'll do my best to keep her after me instead of you."

I squared my puny shoulders and stood up taller under Dad's praise. I was in the second grade and getting this sick baby to the barn was important business. Several of Dad's calves had already died. They came down with pneumonia after being born during a cold spell. Some years were like this—the calves didn't survive infancy. I took it hard. Each little calf meant the world to me. I'd ride out on my pony every day, checking on the herd. I watched John Wayne movies with Dad and imagined myself a real cowboy.

The little calf died the next day even though Dad gave it a shot of penicillin and we did our best to warm it up with blankets and straw. I cried until Dad told me tears were for babies.

"Big girls don't cry," he said, and I believed him.

I wiped my nose and headed to the barn to saddle up my pony. I ran her hard all over the pasture, until she was dripping with sweat and the tears had dissolved inside me, even though it was raining. Maybe heaven was crying for the baby calves.

"You shouldn't ride your pony so hard," Dad said when I finally returned to the house.

Pulling a chair from the table over to the counter, I got the whiskey bottle down from the cabinet. I had just turned eight years old but could make highballs with the best of them. Dad's glass was empty in the kitchen, and I had emptied myself of tears.

"Not too much 7-Up," Dad said, as I stirred his drink and poured the rest of the soda into a blue Tupperware cup for myself, so we could both forget about the calf we couldn't save.

When I looked into my boss's eyes in that Reno hotel room a decade later, I knew he didn't want me, not the way a hot-blooded man wants a woman. All the guys who worked at the restaurant said he was gay. They said the same thing about all our bosses—three rich guys who showed up one day in their Corvettes and took over the restaurant not long after I was hired there. Some days I thought they could be gay, and other days—the times they slept with my female coworkers at the chic hotel they lived in—I didn't think they were. It made me mad that the guys at the restaurant bashed on gays.

My uncle John, whom my brother and I just called Uncle, was gay. He and his partner Ray rode Tennessee Walking horses around their sprawling ranch in the Sierra Nevada foothills. For Christmas one year, they gave me Earth, Wind, & Fire records in a fancy, foldout holder. At nine years old, I couldn't connect with the music. The album *You Light Up My Life* by Debbie Boone was more my style. But I did appreciate their seeing me as worthy of this grown-up gift.

A few years later, Uncle humiliated me when I walked into Christmas wearing a pretty holiday dress and he exclaimed, "Look, everyone, little Paula grew chi-chis this year!"

In the seventh grade, you don't want to hear this, especially when Uncle's exuberant gay friends howled with laughter as I ran for his bathroom to sit with the birds—beyond the tub was a sliding glass door and the bird sanctuary. Feathers flew all over the place when you entered the loo. The birds couldn't fly past the sliding glass door, but they watched you, which made it hard to go to the bathroom. Have you ever been eyeballed by canaries while taking a pee? Uncle also had a monkey named Chimpy. Like Uncle, Chimpy could be a stinker too. She weighed about forty pounds, looked like a troll with a baboon's naked butt, and channeled a junior high girl's knack for cruelty to other females. Ray was her guy. She groomed him regularly, picking through his hair as we sat around the living room after holiday dinners.

My uncle had the gift of hospitality, and Thanksgivings and Christmases tended to be celebrated at his house—an eccentric old Victorian mansion on the ranch, where naked Greek statues adorned a sweeping yard filled with palms, oak trees, and blooming orange trumpet vines. The cats, the dogs, and I all feared Chimpy, especially once I started menstruating, since Chimpy would bite a girl who was on her period. It's as if she had some kind of weird radar. She would also bite her own hand. I have no idea why.

Sitting off by herself in one of her dark moods, Chimpy's hand would begin to twitch. She would look at her twitching hand out of the corner of her eye like it was something she didn't want to scare away. First her hand would twitch, then Chimpy would twitch. Suddenly, she'd shove the hand into her mouth and chew wildly. As if she were killing something that threatened her. She'd also do this when she was mad at you, taking out her aggression on herself.

Chimpy had issues, but don't we all?

My bosses in Reno had issues, maybe because they were young, rich, and arrogant as the day was long. My uncle was rich too, but not like this—not *entitled* rich. Uncle grew up barefoot in summertime because his parents—my paternal grandparents, John and Helen—couldn't afford shoes for him and his brothers (my dad was one of the shoeless), and that barefoot little boy inside him remained there for the rest of his life.

The winsome part of Uncle.

My bosses were "born with a silver spoon in their mouths," as Grandpa John would say about inherited wealth that spoiled people. One of the bosses was the grandson of a well-known hotel magnate, kind of a Conrad Hilton, and I wasn't used to "I want this," and "I'll take this," and "Hold on a minute, I need to light another cigarette and blow smoke in your face before I can talk to you" rich.

You know—stupid rich.

Stupid rich was about to make me do something I didn't want to do. Something that really scared me. The way Dad's old bull had scared me. Still, I rode around that old bull plenty of times, confident I was fast enough to outrun him on my pony and determined to look out for those little calves in Dad's pasture. And at nineteen years old, I was determined to take care of myself in Reno.

Chapter Two

> Years of love have been forgot
> in the hatred of a minute.
>
> — Edgar Allan Poe

I stood on my great-grandfather's porch holding a pony. A living, trotting Shetland I'd led up the front steps. I held the reins in my hand, you can see my diaper in the butt of my pants in the old photograph. I might have been two years old. There was a strap around the pony's withers. That's all—no saddle. I remember holding on to this leather strap for dear life. My grandparents owned a horse stables, and I was put on ponies before I could walk. I never had to ride in the corrals like the other kids. I was allowed to take my pony all over the place. Grandma Helen believed you were safer on top of a horse than under its feet, so that's where she kept me. The pony was my babysitter.

When I rode up to his porch, my great-grandpa, a tiny man older than dirt, would come out and give us both treats. Sugar cubes I dissolved in my mouth as my pony nibbled her sugar off great-grandpa's wrinkled hand. I don't quite remember this, but in a way I do. The old photo proves what Grandma Helen told me: "Nobody could ride like you when you were a baby. From the moment I put you on a pony, you were fearless. The problem was you ruined ponies. You taught them to run, and then other kids couldn't handle them."

It's the only thing I ever remember my grandma chastising me about. I was her pride and joy. She was always showing me off to her friends. "Look at my little granddaughter ride," she'd say so proudly, standing there with her cowboy hat covering her ebony hair, a colorful silk scarf tied around her smooth, white neck. Then she would wave me around the arena on my pony like a band leader conducting a band. My grandma was a blue-eyed beauty with fair, creamy skin, narrow hips, a trim waist, and double-D breasts. She kept her shoulders rolled back so her breasts stuck out like torpedoes on a ship. The stable was her domain. She commanded the operation with grinning ease. Grandpa John saddled Grandma Helen's fine Tennessee Walkers and fixed anything that broke. I remember him always with a hammer in his hand.

I didn't like upsetting Grandma Helen, but I wasn't thinking about other kids when I was running my pony across the pasture hellbent for leather by the time I was four years old. I thought I was an Indian warrior and often let out a loud war whoop as I'd seen braves on their painted ponies do in the movies. The war cry made me feel invincible until the day I was whooping for all I was worth and swallowed a large moth.

My pony was running as fast as she could run, and I was hollering like a banshee, when suddenly that big old moth flew up from the grass and hit the back of my throat. To save myself, I swallowed it. I know it was a moth because the powder from its wings stayed in my mouth. I never whooped again on my pony. But I rode ponies, and later horses, too hard for years. Horses bore the brunt of my emotions. When I was happy, I ran my pony. When I was mad or sad, I ran her harder. Some people drink or do drugs to dull their pain. I consumed ponies.

In Reno, Danny blew smoke in my face before he ordered me to do the line of cocaine after everyone else had done theirs. We were in his hotel room: me and Sara and our other boss, Larry, along with Jules. That's what we called our manager at the restaurant: Jules. It wasn't her real name, but she had jewel-like eyes, as green as emeralds, sly and catlike under her shaggy auburn hair. Like Danny, she always blew smoke in your face before she talked to you. I knew she was sleeping with Danny. Sara was sleeping with Larry. I wondered if Danny and Larry were getting it on too. I hadn't thought that right off the bat. I'd always been naïve this way. People really weren't having sex all over the place. Only parents did it in their bedrooms.

My sophomore year of high school, when one of my friends told me those little pills she took every morning were for allergies, I believed her even though my other friends said they were for birth control, that everyone was taking birth control, and I should too. I was fifteen years old. Who needs birth control at this age? High school kids really didn't sleep together, did they?

"Jules and Sara sleep with those guys for cocaine," a snotty kid who worked at the restaurant told me. I didn't believe him. Jules and Sara, especially Sara, had become my friends. I hung out with them at night after we got off work. This, he told me the second month of my living in Reno on my own. The first month, I just worked and went to college and cried myself to sleep every night in my studio apartment all decorated pink—pink bedspread, old pink trunk I'd painted myself in my parents' garage before moving to Nevada. The trunk sat at the foot of my bed filled with my journals and favorite books. Novels by Jack London. Ernest Hemingway. Edgar Allan Poe. I loved these male writers. Their style was often brutal but beautiful—the way I found life to be. I was an English major and carried books and writing pads everywhere I went.

Pink curtains and rugs and dishes in my apartment.

"Everything's pink in here," said my ex-boyfriend.

He'd stopped by after driving over the mountains that separated California from Nevada on his way to visit the university he would attend that autumn. The same university I was currently attending for spring semester.

"I've missed you," Scott said before kissing me. Pulling me close and molding his body against mine. He tasted like California, all sunshine, sweaty muscles, and spearmint gum.

Oh, how I missed California.

I let him spend the night, and we made love twice before he left the next morning. He didn't call after that—at least for a long, painful time didn't contact me at all.

"None of us are leaving here until Paula does her line," Danny said that night in the hotel.

He was sitting there holding a razor blade white with cocaine, and I think if we were alone, he might have used the blade on my throat. I knew he didn't like me, and everything suddenly made sense. Sara and Jules's erratic behavior since they'd started hanging out with Danny and Larry. My friends' stories that didn't add up. The cash in their pockets they'd gamble away that couldn't have come from their restaurant tips. None of us made that kind of money waitressing.

This moment in the hotel with Danny ordering me to do coke didn't descend on me overnight like a harvest I hadn't farmed myself. It took three months to ripen, the way fruit ripened on the trees in California in those orchards that knew me barefoot as a little girl and broken as a teenager with mascara and tears drenching my face because someone hurt me in an orchard. But I'll tell you more about that later. It's a hard story to share.

For now, I'd grown friendships with Sara, Jules, and Larry. I didn't consider Danny a friend but spent nearly every day working with him at the restaurant. After my morning college classes and then work, I would go out with this group to the casinos. I'd convinced myself this risky lifestyle wouldn't hurt me. I could handle myself. Just a little taste of forbidden fruit was all I wanted.

Sara was a tiny brunette with an angelic face. She looked all of twelve years old but, like me at nineteen, had a fake ID and a winning smile. Also like me, she'd been burned by men. Not just boyfriends but father figures too. Her mom was on her third marriage to a rich doctor in Carson City.

The drill after work went like this: Sara and I arrived at our favorite casino bar near the restaurant. I'd grab my stool at the sports bar, my favorite chair in front of my favorite bartender. I always wondered if that meant the man behind the counter had to be tender to those seated there. In this case, it was true. Carlos, married in his thirties, all handsome Spanish swag—swag, a word not even in my vocabulary yet—was always so tender with me.

Sara was tender with me too. We'd become friends quickly, worked together and played together. I'd never done drugs, and when Sara asked me if I had, the answer flew from my mouth. "I will never do drugs! I could never disappoint my parents that way."

"I love cocaine, but I don't use it anymore. It took me to a bad place." Sara's eyes shone with regret.

We talked about her boyfriends—the boys and men who'd used her. A long list of heartbreaks that made Sara more than sympathetic to my first heartbreak so fresh in my life.

"You really should get rid of that picture," she said about my ex-boyfriend's photo beside my bed in a little round white ceramic frame.

He held my dog Doca, a happy beagle, while smiling wide and appearing endearing with deep dimples in his cheeks. Such a rare picture. Almost every photo I had of Scott wasn't of him smiling, especially wide open this way. He wasn't a wide-open guy.

"Looking at that every morning isn't good for you. You need to let him go," Sara said.

"I know," I answered, picking up an apple slice and sticking it on a piece of Colby cheese.

Sara had taught me this trick beside her parents' pool under the piercing Nevada sun with the Sierra Nevada range stretched all jagged and snow-covered in the distance—that barrier between me and California. Between the land of orchards and the desert of sagebrush. Between my ex's crooked smile and my carved-up broken heart.

Sara was teaching me a lot of things.

"He stops by, sleeps with you, and then doesn't call?" Thin, tan, and beautiful in her tiny little bikini, Sara crunched her apple, scrutinizing me with her stare. We were growing so close, baring our souls, sharing our dreams, frolicking in a field of what-ifs and how can-we-create-the-lives-we-longed-for. Above all, I longed for what I had with Scott before he dumped me.

"I don't know what I'm going to do once he moves here. I hope the university is big enough for both of us." The junior college in California we attended a semester together certainly wasn't big enough. Not when I walked past girls he'd slept with after breaking up with me. I wanted to sleep with someone else too, to get even, but the thought turned my stomach.

"What's it like to be with different guys?" I asked, unashamed of my lack of experience. I just couldn't imagine sleeping around, though I knew kids did. I still found it hard to believe Scott could make love to someone else after us. That kind of intimacy wasn't like mayonnaise. Spreading it around seemed so wrong. And had ripped my heart apart.

"Lonely," she said. "I want to find just one guy to spend the rest of my life with. I want to get married. Have kids. Cook my husband dinner every night wearing an apron of lace. I'm old-fashioned that way."

"Me too." I tried to envision the apron of lace. "I just want to write books and have babies like Danielle Steel. She has like seven kids or something." Seven kids sounded so fun. I loved children and couldn't wait to be a mom.

Sara and I listened to U2 24/7. We blasted it on the stereo of my little blue Toyota Celica with the sunroof gaping open as we sang "With or Without You" as loud as we could, while driving back and forth between Reno and Carson City to lie by the pool and eat apples and cheese. I also sunbathed by my apartment's pool that was too cold to swim in, turning my white skin red, and finally pinkish brown with a thousand more freckles. I'd always hated my freckles. Scott had once tried to kiss every freckle on my back, assuring me my red hair and freckles were sexy. I didn't believe him.

"Marry someone who loves you. Really loves you," said Sara. "My mom's been through the wringer with men. I don't want us to end up like her."

My parents weren't divorced, but I'd recently seen the movie *War of the Roses* and cried the whole way through. That was my parents. I feared they'd do each other in before divorcing. I suspected they'd allowed me to move to Reno to get me out of the house so they could murder each other. They paid for my apartment and college classes, and I covered the rest of my living expenses. Mom drove me over the mountains in Dad's pickup truck full of secondhand stuff she'd collected and stored in our barn for years as she waited for my brother and me to need it in college.

Everything except for my bed. The bed came from my grandpa John. It had a deep dent in the middle of the mattress from his heavy frame. My grandparents had sold the stables, retired on a small ranch, and now lived in a trailer that once belonged to the writer Janet Dailey so they could travel.

"This trailer is a sign," Grandma Helen informed me. "You need to write books like Janet Dailey."

While Grandma Helen read her Dailey lit, Grandpa John fought colon cancer and grew skinnier by the day. In their trailer they headed down to the Salton Sea in November after Thanksgiving to be with other snowbirds—old people wealthy enough to leave winter behind so their bones didn't ache in the cold. When the weather warmed up, they returned to the foothills north of Sacramento.

Grandpa John told my dad, "This dying is a hard business."

He accepted Jesus on his deathbed in the trailer. I saw heaven on his face the day before he died when I drove from Reno for a couple of hours to sit with him in California and hold his hand. When I told him I loved him, Grandpa John didn't answer me back; the cancer had stolen his voice. But his bright-blue eyes shone with heavenly light.

Now in my studio apartment, I had Grandpa John's bed with the dent in the middle. In the small studio the king-size frame barely fit. Sara had taken to sleeping there with me most nights instead of driving back to Carson City, where her mom and stepdad lived in a mansion facing the mountains. This was before California's big drought when the snow didn't all melt away in the summertime. Snow survived within the shadows of the high ridges, cold and frozen—like my ex-boyfriend in my heart.

I just couldn't get over Scott, but I sure was trying with my fake ID that got me into Reno's bars and casinos. I wasn't lost yet but was a long way from home, and my path was growing darker.

Chapter Three

> Every saint has a past, and
> every sinner has a future.
>
> — Oscar Wilde

When almond orchards bloom, it looks as if the trees are covered in snow. Almond blossoms are white and about the size of popcorn. They smell so sweet. As the petals drop, pushed out by incoming leaves, the ground is blanketed in white satin petals for several weeks. If the weather gets too cold during the bloom, farmers run sprinklers in the orchard. They used to burn smudge pots, and all the farm boys would have to fill the smudge pots with oil and light them to warm up the trees. But by the time I turned ten, sprinklers were installed by the farmers and water was used to keep the blossoms from freezing.

It was during the bloom that Scott broke up with me. I packed up to move amid the smell of blooming almonds. Along with my parents' almond orchard, all my parents' neighbors raised almonds too. People came from miles around to take pictures of the stunning orchards, to stand in the intoxicating smell of spring, while I drove away to a land locked in winter.

I was just months out of high school.

I'd met Scott my senior year, the week after my eighteenth birthday. He was a freshman at the local junior college, there to play football and get his grades up enough to move on to a university. When I first saw him in his black leather jacket and torn Levi's long before torn jeans were in style, I couldn't take my eyes off of him.

He looked at me the same way.

We were at a small party with Bon Jovi's "Livin' on a Prayer" blasting on the stereo. I was actually there on a blind date with someone else, a baseball player with a wad of tobacco in his mouth, but I was immediately smitten with Scott and kept looking over at him across the room. He didn't really try to talk to me because I was with that other guy, but his gaze ate me up. Like I was the most delicious thing he'd ever seen. I wanted to taste him too.

A few weeks later, we found each other through a mutual friend that reintroduced us and we immediately became a couple, though I didn't let him kiss me right away. We stood in the rain talking on a full moon night instead of going inside to join a college party. I know, how was the moon out in the rain? It just was, the clouds leaving holes for the moon to shine through. I wasn't about to step foot into that wild party, and Scott was more than happy to get wet with me as we got to know each other. Our conversation flowed so easily. We talked for hours as a soft rain soaked us, and I fell hard and fast for this boy who'd been all over the world. I'd hardly been out of my hometown. But that summer, after my high school graduation, Scott broke up with me. He wanted to mess around with other girls and told me this as if I should be proud of him that he was setting me free after I'd given him my virginity four months into our new relationship. He wasn't a cheater, he said. "I will always tell you the truth. I don't want to be tied down. I want to have sex with other girls again."

I cried a lot that long, hot summer. And took two jobs. Work has always been a refuge for me. But by autumn Scott wanted me back. He found me in the college library and sweet-talked me among the books. I find books incredibly sexy. To be romanced in a library was beyond my endurance. I was taking college classes at the JC, and he kept after me, finding me in the nooks and crannies of the library where I tried to hide from him. At first, I'd walk away because my heart was so shredded, but within a month, I quit one of my jobs to make time for Scott. I couldn't wait to be his girlfriend again, though his wild summer with other girls had crushed me.

Upon getting back together, we went to a college party. Everyone was playing drinking games. I was the youngest there but did my best to keep up. I can't remember the exact details—the night is fuzzy in my mind, but the emotions aren't fuzzy; they are sharp and jagged and still hurt. I remember how I felt that night—young, dumb, and eager to be loved—as we piled into a car with a group of guys to go to another party. A second carload of college kids followed us. When we started driving, I knew that was it for me.

"I'm going to throw up," I told the driver. He stopped the car, and I jumped out. Why I chose to throw up all over myself in the middle of the beaming headlights is beyond me. But that's what I did. Even writing about this now, decades later, I find it a little hard to breathe. I was trying to be one of the cool kids and failing badly that night.

Some of the guys got out of the two vehicles to see what was happening. Maybe they were laughing at me, or maybe they were concerned for me. I really can't remember. But after throwing up all over myself, I tore my sweater off. By then Scott was at my side in the middle of the bright lights. I threw my sweater on the ground because of the vomit. He ripped off his tan flannel shirt and wrapped it around me. The shirt was from Maine—why do I remember this? He'd done his first year of high school there. It felt so warm and soft and big. Bigger than my shame. I'd never been so thankful for a shirt in my life. Scott stood there naked from the waist up on that crisp autumn night. He spent a lot of time in the gym and had amazing muscles. He went without a shirt for over an hour and never complained once, though he had to have been cold.

He called off the party for us. Drove me across two rivers, over several bridges, all the way to the Sutter Buttes, where he snuck me up my parents' stairs and put me to bed with a glass of water. I didn't think I could ever face those college kids again after they saw me drunk. Saw my bra. And my vomit. But Scott said, "You're my girlfriend. Who cares what people think? You're with me."

Now I was no longer with him, I belonged to myself again, and springtime in California felt like the worst time for a breakup. Everything's in bloom. Bees are pollinating all over the place. Birds are mating on the fence every five minutes. The roosters are running the hens ragged. But I was determined to show everyone, especially myself, that I didn't need a boyfriend. I could make it on my own. I would have to replace my cowboy boots with snow boots, but that was the easy part of moving. Leaving California's blooming orchards for a snowy Nevada desert that grew casinos instead of blossoms would be harder.

Two months later, in Reno with the snow melting on the sidewalks, my favorite bartender, Carlos, drove Sara and me home after serving us strawberry daiquiris spiked with Everclear alcohol. That night, my brain went foggy, and I laughed when Sara tilted backward on her barstool and fell, landing with a thud on her back, and out cold on the casino floor. Then I got scared, my thoughts all thick like wet cotton as I knelt beside her, holding her hand, calling her name. People continued to gamble as if it was perfectly normal for a girl to sprawl unconscious beside the ringing, clanking slot machines.

"I'm sorry. I wanted to get you drunk to get to know you better." As Carlos carried Sara and then me into my apartment because we were too drunk to walk, he confessed to spiking our drinks. "You don't belong in Reno. You should go home to your farm."

Carlos put me on Big John's bed and kissed my forehead, his lips lingering there. Sara was already throwing up in my bathroom. Soon, I joined her, and we threw up like puppies nursing side by side, leaning over that milky white toilet bowl, heaving our guts out with the stench of rotten alcohol in the air.

How could Carlos have spiked our drinks? I thought I could trust him. I felt so gullible. And wronged.

"You should go home to your wife," I told Carlos that night, mad and sad all at once.

After two months of frequenting his sports bar nearly every night— Carlos protecting me from prowling men, making me weak drinks I could handle, encouraging me to sip iced milk or Pepsis with a cherry on top, to not lose my sweet, freckled farm-girl way—he'd betrayed me.

After that, I never trusted him again and learned how to handle alcohol I didn't want to consume. Glass in hand, I'd head for the bathroom and dump my drink in a plant as I passed by, wondering if you could get a fern drunk. When I returned to the bar, I'd say, "That drink was good, thanks." Followed by, "No, I'm not ready for another one yet." It was so much easier (and cooler) than saying, "I don't want to drink too much."

I knew keeping my head would keep me out of a man's bed. Drunk girls gave themselves away or got raped—I'd seen enough of that already. I learned to be careful around men, to keep my wits about me.

Carlos only got me drunk that one time; thank goodness Sara was with me that night. After throwing up together for hours and slowly recovering beside the pool in Carson City the next day, she and I grew even closer.

At work I also grew close to the cook, D.J., who invited me over to his trailer a few days after the infamous Everclear adventure. Sara wouldn't give D.J. the time of day.

"He never brushes his hair," she said. "I don't even think he bathes, and he's got a gambling problem."

Sara was funny that way, not wanting to mix with the kitchen workers, but I liked D.J. He had a pregnant wife and four little kids at home. I often loaned him money for diapers and groceries because each payday he would disappear to gamble until he lost all his paycheck. It always cost me more than the actual loan because Larry—who would have to cook when D.J. was gone—taught me the kitchen in order to fill in for D.J. so he didn't have to. I hated that hot, greasy kitchen job and wondered why the bosses put up with D.J.'s disappearances. But it was probably for the same reason I always loaned D.J. the cash he needed. He was a likable and otherwise hardworking guy, good at generating plenty of sympathy with his pregnant wife and passel of hungry kids.

So, I went to D.J.'s trailer one afternoon to meet his wife, a slow-on-the-ball girl with a big bow tied in her hair and small children running around half naked though a cold front had blanketed spring snow outside. The trailer was a mess with dishes piled in the sink and ashtrays filled with cigarette butts everywhere.

"I want to look pretty for D.J. during this pregnancy," said the wife as we sat on a dirty sofa with kids crawling around our feet. "He works so hard in that restaurant. The last pregnancy, I let myself go. You should never let yourself go when you're pregnant. Men get to lookin' around, and pretty soon they're sleepin' around."

I nodded sympathetically and told her she had a nice bow, but all I could think was that big pink ribbon belonged in a child's hair. She should stop worrying about looking pretty while pregnant and stop getting knocked up.

D.J. and his friend Dwayne were drinking beer across the trailer at the kitchenette. They sat at the table in mismatched chairs,

Dwayne watching me from under his scruff of dirty-blond hair. He looked like a snowboarder back before I knew what snowboarders looked like.

"That's a nice lamp, D.J.," I called over to them. I didn't want to hear any more about D.J.'s wife's pregnancies and cheating husbands.

"What lamp?" D.J. asked.

"That one." I pointed to a tall hokey-pokey thing on stacked milk crates beside the couch. A lamp made out of a series of blue pipes. I'd never seen anything like it, though I could tell it was homemade, maybe something D.J. pieced together.

Dwayne grinned. "Wow, where'd you find her?" he asked D.J., his voice full of admiration.

"She's from a farm north of Sacramento."

Now Dwayne really stared at me with his brown, puppy-dog, I'll-follow-you-home eyes. "Will you go out with me?" he suddenly asked. He reminded me of D.J.'s wife, kind of simple and slow-witted, maybe a little oxygen-deprived in the airless trailer.

I didn't answer him.

"It's a bong," D.J. said, ignoring Dwayne.

The only kind of bong I'd ever heard of was a beer bong. I'd seen those at high school parties. I could see the fuse where you lit the lamp, but I couldn't figure out how it worked.

"You want to try it with me?" Dwayne asked.

Maybe I was the slow-witted one in the room. I didn't know what Dwayne was talking about trying, but I knew I didn't want to do anything with him.

"It's for weed." D.J. looked a bit sheepish. "I know you're not into that stuff."

I stood up, my knees trembling. "You know, I really need to get going. It's my grocery shopping day."

It was Sunday, and I had the sudden urge to find a Catholic church. Since I'd moved to Reno, I'd stopped going to Mass but still prayed every night. Just one prayer: *Please, God, don't let me have any nightmares.* So far, God had answered that prayer. I hadn't had a nightmare since moving into the apartment by myself, though, at home, I had nightmares often. Sometimes they'd turn into night terrors—I'd wake up and still see the demon of my dreams standing beside my bed. It was terrifying. An unearthly cold swirled around my bedroom when the demon was there. Those nights were the worst. I tried not to think about it, determined to convince myself it was only a nightmare and not something real.

Kind of like *now* ... as I slowly woke to the realization that D.J. was a druggie.

Instead of finding a church after leaving D.J.'s trailer park, I made do with the mall and a new calico kitten I found at a pet shop there. Soon I would appropriately refer to her as *my demon cat.* She made my life hell at home. Something was seriously wrong with her. And my life on the wrong road with the wrong people was about to get me into real trouble.

Chapter Four

>Not until we are lost do we begin
>to understand ourselves.
>
>— Henry David Thoreau

During high school I spent my summers selling tomatoes at farmers' markets and working at my grandparents' farm stand on Highway 99. These were my maternal grandparents, Jack and Anne Phillips. We sold only tomatoes at the stand —Early Girls, Aces, and Celebrities. Everybody wanted the Early Girls. They were the first tomatoes of the season, and people lost their minds over them. I never understood this when I was young. How could you get so excited over a tomato?

"You grow the most amazing homegrown tomatoes I've ever tasted," people would say time and again, and I would respond, "My grandpa, brother Patrick, and cousin Sean grow them out behind the orchard. I just sell them here." The tomatoes were Patrick and Sean's thing. They put themselves through college farming tomatoes, making their sisters, me included, run the stand all summer long and also go to the farmers' market for them. You had to get up really early to sell tomatoes. Especially on the days we drove to Sacramento to set up our market tent beneath a rumbling freeway overpass. We left around 5 a.m. after packing the truck under my grandparents' garage lights.

At the farm stand in front of my grandparents' house, people often asked where we grew the tomatoes. I would point past the peach trees to a rambling garden no one could see from the highway. Sweat would run down my back in the summer heat. I always kept my hair in a ponytail. When I didn't have a customer, my nose was buried in a romance novel. Sometimes dust from the orchard would swirl through the stand if my grandpa was on his tractor. Then I would have to dust off my book and wipe down all the tomatoes. Those high school days moved so slowly, I thought I would never get on with my life. I would live surrounded by tomatoes forever reading torch books—as my dad called the historical romance novels I got from my mom and Grandma Helen.

Near mealtimes, because I was hungry, I would head into the house to help my grandma Anne, who never read a torch book in her life. She was a devout Catholic; those books were way too racy for her. In her kitchen, I would peel long green cucumbers and slice them up, along with fat red tomatoes and sweet yellow onions from the garden, as I watched out the kitchen window for customers coming to the stand. Whenever Grandma Anne made her famous salad dressing, I'd pay close attention. She never followed a recipe. I loved her red wine vinegar, Wesson oil, and squirt of ketchup salad dressing but hadn't been able to duplicate it yet, perhaps because I was young, and it had pinches of this and that, like paprika, sugar, and sweet basil. And who knows what else. My grandma had a lot of spices, plus I was always running out the door to wait on a customer at the stand.

Once I moved to Reno, I bought all the ingredients and tried to make Grandma Anne's salad to comfort myself, but store-bought tomatoes taste terrible, and the grocery store cucumbers weren't much better. Just carrots sliced and marinated in Grandma's dressing was one of my favorite comfort foods, but I couldn't get the dressing right. Maybe Grandma's love was the missing ingredient. I soon gave up on making her salad because all it did was make me homesick, so I turned to learning how to stir-fry instead. I bought a wok with my first paycheck and perfected a Chinese recipe in my four-feet-square kitchen where I taught myself to eat with chopsticks because chopsticks seemed so cosmopolitan; I felt so sophisticated eating food with tiny sticks.

Through half-lidded eyes my cat would watch me prepare Chinese food and fumble with my chopsticks, which made me self-conscious. As if I wasn't a grown-up in my own kitchen. Only pretending to be grown-up and failing at it because that danged cat knew my struggle. Have you ever thought an animal looked down on you? I really think that cat was a demon, mocking me when I used my chopsticks.

A month after my demon cat began despising me in my kitchen, I found myself sitting in a hotel room with cocaine and that razor blade pointed at me. Sara, with white powder coating her nose, watched as I resisted Danny's order to do a line.

"There's a first for everything, Paula," said Sara. "Just do it." She was eagerly waiting for the cash Danny and Larry would hand her and Jules once we reached the casino. Cash they'd stolen from the restaurant's safe just an hour earlier, which had set off the alarm.

We had all jumped into the same car, tires squealing out of the parking lot as a cop car tore in. Danny laughed like a madman while Larry cussed like crazy to cover up his fear.

Someone higher up had the alarm code, probably a rich father of one of these bosses.

Sara had become tight with Jules and rarely spent the night at my apartment anymore. She crashed with the bosses or at Jules's place. I was never invited to Jules's place, probably because of the cocaine. Everyone knew I didn't do drugs.

"It's no big deal. Just do your line so we can get out of here," Sara pushed. "We'll go see Carlos. You can sit at his bar while we gamble."

I did Danny's line in the hotel room with tears in my eyes and my heart pounding out of my chest. After I sucked the powder up my nose, we all headed to the casino. I was shaking, coming out of my skin, becoming someone I'd never met before—someone not afraid of Danny or any other man. I felt ten feet tall as I took the money from Larry and along with Jules and Sara began to gamble with confidence—winning, drinking, winning some more. When I finally made it back to my apartment at five a.m., I was still drunk and high and emboldened.

Coming off the cocaine, booze, and gambling, I began to feel sick. Not just physically but emotionally and spiritually sick as well. I was now crossing lines I swore I'd never cross—white lines cut by a cold-eyed man.

And there was my demon cat, staring at me inhospitably inside my apartment.

I can't even remember what I originally named my calico demon cat, but she was a beast from the beginning, this fierce, little, half-grown thing captured out in the sagebrush somewhere and brought to the pet store to sell to a stupid person like me. Her behavior got so bad I was forced to hang a hammock above my bed to escape her. Instead of loving me like I'd hoped, she terrorized me.

Why did I seem to fall in love with those unwilling to love me back?

Maybe because I was high, I vividly remembered the calico that had once loved me. As a little girl, I stood in front of the sliding glass door, sobbing my heart out as Dad hunted calico kittens out in our barnyard. Calico kittens, wild and fierce and driving me nuts as I tried to tame them. Their mother was tame. Her name was Calico, and she was such a special cat. I loved her so much. The day she had kittens deep in the hay, I spent hours holding her in a chicken's nesting can. The can nailed to the barn wall was full of straw, and I stuck Calico in there and petted and petted her.

The next day, to my delight, she understood what I wanted and moved all her kittens to the nesting can where I could love on them too.

The nesting can didn't last long; the chickens pitched a fit. So Calico moved her brood back to the hay, and that was the end of me taming those kittens. I never could get my hands on them as they grew, and they got wilder and wilder until they instinctively began killing the chickens. This led to the rifle blasts in the barnyard.

Half-grown calico kittens flopping all over the place. Bleeding. Dying. Calico lost a foot in the slaughter.

"I didn't mean to shoot her," Dad said when he finally came in the house.

I was worn out from sobbing at the sliding glass door. Dad was worn out from kitten hunting.

"She got in the way under the barn when I was aiming at a kitten."

"Will Calico die?" I asked as Dad stood there with his rifle draped across his arm.

"I don't know."

"Can we take her to the vet?" I knew it was a dumb question because my parents didn't take animals to the vet. If something got hurt on the farm, Mom nursed it back to health, or Dad grabbed his gun and put the poor thing out of its misery. But Calico did survive, and though she lost all her toes on a front foot, she got around just fine on three feet once she recovered. But deep down, I'm not sure I ever recovered from that bloody day.

So many gun blasts filled my childhood.

Living out in the country with the neighbors a mile or two away, I didn't play much with other kids. The animals were my friends, and I spent most of my time with them—feeding them, loving them, and burying them.

Now, at five a.m. after a night of coke and gambling, my demon calico dumped my purse in the toilet when I got home.

I'd left my purse sitting beside the bathroom sink. I heard the splash and saw her disappear under my bed. Her lair. Sometimes when I walked by barefoot, she'd slice my foot open with her claws. I was covered in bites and scratches. It was like having a cobra for a roommate.

With my purse in the pooper, I suddenly hated my pink apartment. With the residue of cocaine burning in my nose, I suddenly hated my life.

What was I becoming in Reno?

"You need to go home," Larry had said yesterday morning. "You need to go back to your farm in California. You don't belong in Reno."

"My dad kicked me out," I confessed. "He found out I was sleeping with my boyfriend." Not an earth-shaking event for someone like Larry, but it was to my dad. And to me.

"What happened with the boyfriend?"

"I lived with him for a few days, then he dumped me too."

"That's too bad. You're a good kid." Larry's eyes were compassionate; it made me feel better for a minute.

Both Larry and I stood beside the steaming grill, sweating and reeking of bacon. I'd grown attached to him. He protected me from Danny at the restaurant, especially when Danny was in a foul mood, which was about every day. Larry would send me on some errand in another part of the restaurant when he caught Danny headed my way. It was a big restaurant with a sprawling bar, dance floor, and a bakery and huge kitchen. Like a football field of feeding and entertaining people. If Danny was coming to speak with me, Larry would step between us and start talking business, taking Danny's mind off me. When we were out drinking after work,

Larry would lead Danny away if he saw Danny's eyes resting on me for too long.

When that happened, I could feel Danny's resentment.

One time, Danny said, "You're so f—ing innocent, it's sickening." Then he blew smoke in my face as he stared into my eyes.

I think he knew I hated his smoke, though I never said a word. I just held my breath, smiled, and did what I was told.

But at the hotel earlier that night, Larry didn't say anything when Danny ordered me to do the cocaine. He just stood there silent, his eyes mourning me. I knew he wasn't going to stop Danny anymore. Maybe he couldn't stop him anymore.

Larry had given me a warning in the kitchen that morning. I think he did it to show me why I needed to return to the farm for my own good … my own safety.

Twenty-four hours later, I stood there, scrambling eggs in my studio apartment, pondering my scrambled life with the contents of my purse soaking in the toilet. I hadn't fished it out. I let it sink to the bottom of the bowl. I was too tired and hungry and high to deal with drowning lip gloss, tampons, and the ID of a lost soul.

I was sinking to the bottom too.

Larry had failed me. Carlos had failed me. Why was I always looking for salvation in men? Putting my trust in a man always got me into trouble in the long run. The only reason I started hanging out with Sara, Jules, Danny, and Larry after work was I'd come to trust Larry. He'd turned into something like an older brother to me.

And I was lonely.

Trying to sleep in my Reno studio apartment, I would dream of life on the farm. Calling "Come, boss. Come, girls," in my sleep as Dad had taught me to gather our cows to the barn each day to feed them. When the cows heard me calling, they'd come running like any animal that loved its master's voice.

Perhaps this was God calling me in my dreams. "Come back, come, Girl ...." A plea for me to return to the safety of the farm. In that desperate moment, scrambling those eggs, I suddenly knew I was never going to spend another night alone in this pink apartment with a demon cat. I was losing everything good and right and true in myself here.

I was spiraling out of control.

Leaving the eggs on the stove, I went to fish my driver's license and some money out of the toilet. I'd done okay gambling, and the cash became a wet wad in my pocket.

I threw on my coat and tossed the eggs onto the kitchen linoleum for Demon Cat. Then I walked out the door into the dark, cold, high-desert air. Neon lights blinked in the distance—like the red eyes of the demon of my childhood. Dad flicking his cigarettes out onto the lawn in the dark of night, telling my big brother Patrick, and me that the glowing tip of the cigarettes were the eyes of the Grinch we so feared.

We were just little kids, with our mom often working at the hospital at night. On that note, Dad would put us to bed—terrified. If I cried, he'd come and whip me with his belt.

Now grown up, I was still so afraid of demons. And they were coming after me, those neon-light eyes. I couldn't drive fast enough as dawn approached. As I looked in my rearview mirror, the rising sun over the curve of the mountains blinded me, and I nearly drove off a cliff close to the state line.

Welcome to California.

Cocaine, alcohol, and fear left me shaking and crying behind the wheel. Still, I couldn't go home. Not back to the farm, anyway. Not back to Dad unable to look at me because he was so ashamed that I was no longer a virgin.

And that was before the cocaine.

My parents would be so disappointed if they found out I'd done drugs.

I headed for Scott's apartment because I didn't know where else to go.

Chapter Five

> Sometimes I'm terrified of my heart; of its constant hunger for whatever it is it wants. The way it stops and starts.
>
> — Edgar Allan Poe

Dad roared up to the cabin on his motorcycle with the other dads one Fourth of July afternoon. All the kids played in the meadow while the dads played on their "murdercycles." That's what the wives in the cabins chatting and reading romance novels called the dads' motorbikes when I was little.

The men tore all over the mountains, up and down the dirt logging roads way too fast, far back into the woods to remote lakes filled with rainbow trout. They fished and goofed off, getting drunk while their wives watched the children at the cabins.

"Come here, Paula," Dad called to me from his idling motorcycle in the meadow. "Not you kids ... just my girl," he added when the other kids came too. "I have a surprise for you," he said with love in his eyes and a drunken grin on his face.

He tucked me on the front of the warm motor and took off through the mountains, the wind blowing my long straight hair into Dad's face. He insisted my hair stay long. Mom had short hair, and Dad was always after her to grow it out. She never did. Mom was stubborn that way, unwilling to submit to Dad's authority. It was her hair, after all, she said.

When I was nine, she went against Dad and pierced my ears when he was off deer hunting. He was mad and did some cussing but said as long as we kept my hair long, covering those earrings, he could live with it.

On his next deer hunting trip, Mom took me to her stylist for a Dorothy Hamill haircut that was all the rage back then. My parents had a massive fight over my short bowl-like bob, so I grew it back out. That was my first lesson in asserting myself as a woman like Mom. I would keep my hair long for Dad. It was my hair, after all.

Following the wild ride through the forest, Dad parked the motorcycle and took my hand, walking me deep into the woods.

"Be really quiet," he whispered. "We don't want to scare the mommy if she's around."

I felt so special alone with Dad. He hadn't taken my brother or any of the other kids into the woods. Just me. Only me. Dad's little girl, me.

"What is it?" I asked, instinctively knowing it had to be a baby creature.

I loved baby creatures.

"There," said Dad. "Look right over curled in the grass."

"It's so small," I said in wonder. "It can't be a baby deer; it's too tiny."

But it was a baby deer, the smallest fawn I'd ever seen. Big brown eyes blinked at me. Nothing else moved but those precious eyes looking into mine.

"Man can't touch it, or the mommy will abandon it and it'll die."

Dad sounded so solemn. I smelled the beer on his breath and the wild tang of pines in the air. We stood there holding hands with the wind singing through those woods, smiling at the baby deer for a moment, that image imprinted forever on my mind. It kept me remembering that Dad loved me, though he never told me he loved me. Not once in my whole life.

But now a man had touched me, I'd slept with Scott, and I felt Dad's abandonment. I couldn't go home. My parents didn't want me there. But I was afraid if I stayed in Reno, I'd die.

I drove on to California—to Scott's apartment, where I knocked on Scott's door at seven a.m. His roommate answered in his boxer shorts.

"He's not here," he said, his hair sticking straight up from sleep. He knew exactly who I was looking for.

Tears sprayed down my cheeks. I was on the verge of breaking apart. Coming off the cocaine left me a mess.

"He's not with another girl. He's in Monterey getting dive certified." The roommate closed the door in my face when a girl called his name from inside the apartment.

Feeling absolutely alone, more alone than I'd ever felt in my life, I got back in the car and drove to an apartment down the street where Scott's buddy Aaron lived. I couldn't stop crying—the little fawn facing death.

The death of love.

After knocking on Aaron's door, I stood there sobbing. Where would I go if Aaron wasn't home? What would I do? Just when I was about to leave the building, the door opened.

"Are you okay?" Aaron pulled me into his apartment and closed the door behind us. He was tall and attractive with chocolate brown eyes and dirty blond hair that curled off his forehead. Aaron had seen me throwing up drunk. Seen me fresh from my boyfriend's bed. He'd always been so sweet to me.

He lived with another guy and hurried me through their living room and into his bedroom, shutting that door too. "What happened?"

"I did cocaine."

He grabbed me by the shoulders. "And then what happened?"

"I gambled and drank and drove home from Reno."

He pulled me into his arms, resting his chin on my hair, rubbing my back. "You scared me. I thought something bad happened to you."

Something bad had happened to me.

I cried harder.

The two men I loved most in the world, Dad and Scott—men I thought would take care of me forever—had both forsaken me.

Other men had hurt me. Why couldn't I be strong like my mom? Strong like my grandma? Strong like Great Granny Elizabeth Phillips, who shook her fist at men on the river? This long lineage of women who never cowered to men or needed a man's love.

What had happened to me?

Why was I so different?

Why did I long for a man to love me? Really love me? Perfectly, completely love me?

Love was a crap show. Did anyone survive love?

"You need some sleep." Aaron's brown eyes were full of concern, his handsome face awash in worry. He pulled me over to his twin bed and laid me down with him. I cried myself to sleep in his arms. Hours later, he talked me in to going home. Back to the farm.

That evening, my parents silently accepted me as the sun sank behind the Sutter Buttes and the cows headed for the barn. Dad still refused to look at me, talk to me, or stay in the same room with me. But Mom said, "Now you can go to Chico. I signed you up months ago. You got accepted to the university. You start in the fall. We'll move you there this week, and you can get a job for the rest of the summer."

I stood in church the next day beside my mom that weekend I gave up on Reno. I realized moving home was temporary—I was just passing by the farm. I couldn't stay. I hung my head in shame as the Sunday morning Mass droned on. Above all, I knew God didn't want me, could never want me, sinner that I was. The God of my mothers—the whole mother line that spawned me. Stalwart women of faith married to men who didn't worship God. This had always been a sore spot for me—no men in church with us.

I had grown up at Mass with my mom and my grandma, but never my dad or my grandpa. Dads didn't attend church. White-haired old men nodding to sleep in the pews beside their old blue-haired wives were sometimes there, but no strong, young daddies with their families making the pilgrimage on Sunday mornings.

None except one.

I remember a tall, handsome, dark-haired father with his wife and kids in front of us at Mass when I was in high school. One day, I dreamed this man was my dad, our whole family together just like it should be. I ached for that. To stand with a man in church. In life. A man I could count on. A man I could trust. I may as well have wanted a giraffe to go to church with me.

When would this service be over?

On Monday I got up at zero dark thirty and drove over the mountains for my last week of school in Reno. After class, I called the restaurant to talk with Larry.

"I can't come back," I explained to him. "I'm sorry I missed work on Saturday, but Friday night scared me. I will never do cocaine again. Danny can't make me do it."

Larry more than understood. "I'm so happy for you," he said. "You're back on the farm with your family where you belong."

I didn't tell him I was packing up my pink apartment in Reno as we spoke, trying to corner my demon cat so I could get her to the car.

After my mom and I left church the day before, we'd dropped by my parents' almond farming neighbors, the little old German couple down the road my mom checked on every week. Teresa was out in her flower garden when we got there. Somehow, the conversation came up that I had a wild calico cat in need of a home.

"I'll take her," said Teresa, her white hair silver in the sunlight. "I need a good mouser around here. Wild calicos are the best mousers."

So that's where my demon cat ended up after clawing up my arms as well as the upholstery of my car. I highly recommend kenneling a cat when you're driving on curving mountain roads. She went bat-crap crazy the first half hour of the drive, scrambling around my little Celica like a rabid thing as I did my best to ignore her freaking out. I closed the sunroof and kept going as she slammed herself against the windows trying to escape. What else could I do but drive? Finally, she wedged herself under my driver's seat and getting her out at Teresa's house took patience and a broom.

Driving back and forth through the mountains every day for a week after that, I finished my semester at the university and cleared out my apartment, set on never doing cocaine again. Never living in Reno again. Never owning a cat again. And so thankful Scott wasn't home when I went to his apartment that dark morning, feeling like I had nowhere else to go.

But just a month later, with my fake ID and new friends in California, I found myself doing cocaine again.

What was it going to take for me to escape my own demons?

Chapter Six

When the world says, 'Give up,' hope whispers, 'Try it one more time.'

— Unknown

At nineteen all I wanted was to "Dance with Somebody Who Loves Me." You couldn't get out of a club without hearing that Whitney Houston song. You couldn't get into a club without an ID either. My fake one worked every time.

My new friends—all college students in their twenties—were older than me. They came from middle-class families, not rich but certainly not poor. They could afford a little cocaine, but I was still shocked to find they had some. Not nearly as much cocaine as my bosses in that Reno hotel room.

I remember thinking at first that Danny was cutting lines of salt—that he'd taken a big salt shaker from the restaurant and was messing with it on the hotel room desk.

The friend who had the cocaine in California had only a few vials; they looked like little medical vials filled with powder he poured out on his dorm desk. He had graduated that week, and a group of us at his university were celebrating before we left for the club. I felt like such a little girl around them.

I wasn't even of legal drinking age yet, but nobody seemed to mind.

"Have you ever seen coke?" one of them asked me.

There I stood in a long-fitted denim skirt with my hair all permed, pulled back in a banana clip, and my freckled skin tan for a change. A real change since I think this was the only genuine tan I'd ever had, thanks to a summer of burning myself under the Nevada sun.

"I've seen a lot more coke than this," I said, surprising everyone.

"Have you tried coke?" one of them dubiously asked.

Nobody in that room expected such brazen behavior from me.

I began to tremble, wanting that coke really bad, yet, not wanting it really bad. I didn't want to do drugs ever again, knowing what cocaine would do for me—remove my fear and give me dangerous confidence. But I needed that confidence if I was going to use my fake ID to get into a popular downtown dance club on graduation week in this university town. A club everyone said was really hard to get into when you're not of age because they watched for minors trying to slip in under the radar.

"I did coke in Reno," I admitted as the magical snow was cut into lines on the dorm room desk.

"Well, way to go, Paula!" said a friend with a Corona beer in hand, making fun of that *An Officer and a Gentleman* movie dialogue.

"You can do the first line since you're the youngest," said another friend holding the razor blade.

So, I did it first and then sailed into that club like the Queen of Sheba and danced my fanny off, oblivious to the fact that I only really knew how to two-step to country music. But cocaine has a way of turning you into your wildest, freest self—the way you dream of being—if only in your head.

I danced like a gypsy in my long Levi skirt, losing my banana hair clip somewhere on the dance floor, before doing more cocaine in the bathroom stall with my friends. Laughing our inhibitions away. Spraying Obsession perfume in each other's faces. Dancing until the bar closed down.

But I didn't find somebody to love me that night. Not surprising since I was still hopelessly in love with Scott, though I hadn't seen or talked to him since he stopped by my apartment in Reno that one time to make love to me and then never called me again.

I danced for hours with a dozen different guys and ended up at a fraternity house, where I crawled out a bathroom window sometime around four a.m. because I didn't want to end up in bed with somebody I didn't love. My friends crashed at the frat house doing God-knows-what with God-knows-who as I walked several blocks in the dark to find my car. I was still so coked up, I didn't have sense enough to be scared alone in the night.

It was all backroads driving the hour and a half home—nothing but farm fields shadowed by the deep blue horizon, like the bruise of dawn before the light. And I felt so bruised myself, living in a shadowland of things I knew were wrong. In my car I was still half drunk, half high, the girl from high school who'd signed a pledge never to do drugs. To never drive drunk. I'd lost friends in drunk-driving accidents. Now, I was behind the wheel.

I knew how serious drunk driving was. How serious cocaine was. And, again, I wondered how I'd gotten to this point. I felt so lost.

I couldn't blame Reno anymore. It was me. I was the problem.

Around dawn, I drove past my grandparents' farm on Highway 99. Their kitchen light was on, and I started crying. Grandma Anne was up fixing Pop's breakfast. Grandpa Jack—we kids just called him Pops—was a peach farmer, and his day started early. Normally, I would honk when I passed their house—all the grandkids honked. But not this morning.

Brokenness had invaded my soul. Deep down inside I had a need for something that would make me what I wasn't: a strong woman. A woman like my mom. She'd say no to cocaine. No to drunk driving. No to sex before marriage.

I felt shame passing my grandparents' house with the kitchen light on like a beacon of all I wasn't anymore. The yard Grandma Anne kept immaculate with the Santa Rosa plum tree I loved in the corner. The tree I climbed, sat on a limb, and ate plums until my stomach ached. A row of carefully tended rosebushes bloomed along the front porch. In their backyard stood a towering sycamore tree.

I adored that white-barked sycamore. In the moonlight, it reminded me of a naked woman, its bark smooth and white and lovely. A clothesline stretched out past the sycamore tree, Grandma's cotton blouses, Bermuda shorts, and Pop's Levi's blowing in the delta breeze. My grandparents' backyard reminded me of how life moved slow and steady and sure on the farm. A place where kids never had to try drugs or drive drunk or lose their way because the old way was there.

Life on the farm was still there.

That Sunday I went to Mass with my mom, my cocaine binge fresh in my mind. I felt so guilty. I asked God to forgive me for losing my way and to please help me never, ever do cocaine again. Because I liked it—really, really liked it.

I could live on that stuff.

But I didn't want to get hooked on drugs. And didn't want life on the farm either. Not after grading peaches in my grandparents' orchard every summer for years and sweating at the farmers' market selling tomatoes. I couldn't wait to leave that rural life behind, and I couldn't wait to speed past my grandparents' place without honking the horn because I knew I was broken.

More than anything, I wanted to escape. I didn't know who I was anymore and wasn't sure where I'd go, but I knew a farm couldn't hold me.

Still, I wanted a man to hold me. Someone good. Someone true. Someone I could trust for the rest of my life.

Chapter Seven

To the girl I was then: I forgive you.

— Unknown

Chico State University was ranked the #1 party school by *Playboy* when I moved there after leaving Reno that summer before I turned twenty. I took a waitressing job in a downtown café, making coffee at five a.m. for construction guys before they headed off to their job site. Though they were all big, strapping, sunburnt men, they carried Bibles under their arms into the restaurant. Unlike men I was used to, none of them stared at my breasts or patted my behind or flirted as I served them each morning. They always looked straight into my eyes and smiled with compassion. I didn't want to like these Christians who read their Bibles while drinking coffee, but I soon grew attached to them.

"It must be hard to only get a few hours of sleep before coming to work," said Chris, a thirty-something man with muscles acquired from hard work, not the gym. He waited until I filled his coffee cup before admitting, "I used to party in this town too. I don't miss getting drunk. I've found something better."

"Jesus is better than anything you'll ever find." Tom, a younger guy with his own sunburnt neck and arms, joined the conversation.

I nodded and smiled, uncomfortable with their Jesus talk as I filled Tom's cup.

"I'm Catholic. I'm good," I said as I rounded the table, priming their cups as I did every weekday morning. I used to refill fast to get away from them but now took my time. These men intrigued me. I felt safe with them and liked hearing them talk about the Bible.

"Why don't you come to our church this Sunday? It's just across town. We have a college group you might enjoy."

"I only go to the Catholic Church." I quickly finished refreshing their coffees and left in a hurry. Now they were inviting me to church. Yikes!

"I'm Catholic. I'm good," I insisted again the following day.

And again, the next day when they didn't give up on me coming to their church. "I'm Catholic. I don't go to other churches. My grandma would have a fit."

"Jesus isn't a religion. Jesus loves you. We are all praying for you, Paula."

To my surprise, tears rushed to my eyes when the guys said they were praying for me. My head pounded from the Tequila shots I'd done the night before. I still had sawdust in my sandals from the bar where you could spit your peanut shells on the floor while you listened to country music. Though I was making friends in Chico, none of those college friends prayed for me. Somehow, these guys looked right into my heart and saw my deepest need. I wanted to be loved, but while they were trying to win me over, I was stacking bricks around my heart as fast as I could. I needed a wall to keep men out. Guys at school wanted to date me, but I turned them all down.

"Between work and college, I don't have time for dating" was my standard answer, which I always shoveled gently. I knew it took courage to ask a girl out and didn't want to make anyone feel bad. Except the creeper at the counter who kept calling me Pamela, though I'd told him my name a hundred times.

Of course I had a creeper in my life. Since the seventh grade I'd always had some guy acting weird with me. The creep at the counter drank cup after cup of coffee, staring at me with emotionless eyes, holding his cup up for a refill again and again. My fear of him was growing. He usually came in after my construction guys left, but one morning he showed up when they were still studying their Bibles.

"Is that guy a problem for you?" Chris asked, pointing to the counter, without his normal smile when I went over to see if they wanted another round of coffee.

"He's just strange," I tried to brush it off as no big deal.

"Why does he call you Pamela?"

"I don't know. I've told him my name enough times." I pointed to my name tag on my waitress uniform. "The guy is just weird. He never eats. Only drinks gallons of coffee and stares at people."

Mostly at me. But I didn't tell Chris that.

This was the story of my life. I had a stalker. Maybe I was too nice to creeps. The world could be a lonely place. Smiling was easy and made people feel better. The prettiest thing a girl could wear was a smile, but I no longer smiled at the creep at the counter. He made my skin crawl.

Chris stood up, towering over me. His work shirtsleeves were rolled up to his elbows. Muscles ripped under his skin. He gently touched my shoulder.

"I'll take care of it."

He walked over to the counter and sat down beside the creep.

I hurried to the kitchen, not wanting to be around for whatever happened. When I returned, the counter was empty. Chris and his friends were gone and so was the creeper.

The next day, Chris and two other construction guys lingered at their table until the creeper came in. When I got up the courage, I walked over to serve the creep.

"Good morning, Pamela." His emotionless eyes flashed fire. That surprised me. "Why don't you like me? You like those meatheads over there."

He didn't look toward Chris's table, but I knew exactly whom he meant.

My knees began to tremble. I'd told my boss, who cooked in the kitchen, that this guy at the counter disturbed me, but my boss thought he was harmless.

"He's a regular. Don't worry about him," said my boss.

I tried not to worry but was on the verge of quitting—not just because of the creep, but also it was now September and school was loading up on me. If I went to school full-time, my parents wouldn't make me work. Their priority was for me to graduate as quickly as possible. I didn't have to keep this waitressing job.

Work boots thudded on the floor behind me. I spun around as Chris took a seat at the counter. His large sun-burnished hands were a stark contrast to the guy's thin, pasty fingers around his coffee cup. Chris's friends filed out the door, calling goodbyes as they left. I looked at Chris, but he wasn't budging from his stool. He gave me a reassuring smile and calmly sipped his coffee.

I headed to the kitchen to fill some orders. When I returned, Chris and the creep were gone.

The creep never returned, and I never asked Chris what he'd done to make him leave. I was just grateful nobody at the counter called me Pamela anymore. Before working at that cafe, I didn't like in-your-face Christians, but Chris and his friends had won me over. When I told them I was quitting a couple of weeks later, I burst into tears.

"I'll miss you guys. Thanks for being so nice to me early in the morning. I'm not a morning person."

"We'll be praying for you," they all said as they hugged me goodbye. That night I went out to the bars with my fake ID and got hammered.

Once I quit my job, I partied even more because I didn't have to get up early for work. I began to spend a lot of time with a new group of friends, and we drank most nights. By October standing in an old Spanish-style Catholic Church with the sun streaming through stained-glass windows, trees blazing orange, yellow, and red in Chico, I asked the Lord to rescue me.

"Please save me from this wild college life. I don't want to be this alcohol-reeking, regretful person any longer," I prayed.

I got so drunk the night before at a party, I found myself in bed with Aaron—that attractive, brown-eyed guy who'd comforted me after the cocaine-fueled night I ran home from Reno. Aaron had shown up at a party. I was so surprised to see him in Chico. He came right to my side and together we drank our inhibitions away. Before I awoke the next morning, Aaron had disappeared. When I recovered enough from my hangover to get out of bed, I found that church to cry in and confess my mess. I just felt so empty inside after that night. Like I had poured all my sorrow over Scott into Aaron. Now I just wanted it all to go away. I never wanted to see Aaron again.

But a few days after that, he called and asked me to meet him so we could talk. I told him he could come to my apartment, but when he got there, I ran right outside to his Chevy because I didn't want to invite him inside ever again. Both of us were embarrassed by what we'd done. And Aaron was so filled with guilt, he couldn't stand it.

"I need to tell Scott what happened between us. I can't keep this secret from him. I don't know when I'll tell him, but I have to tell him. I know he really loved you," Aaron said, which was so dumb. If you really love someone, you don't leave. Scott had dumped me nine months earlier.

Still, Aaron wanted forgiveness for crossing a line neither of us should have crossed, and everything in me longed for forgiveness too, but it didn't seem possible. I couldn't imagine Scott would forgive me for sleeping with Aaron. Maybe he was so done with me, he wouldn't even care.

"You do what you have to do." I was relieved this bird was out of its cage.

The big black crow squawking and pecking in the tree above us there in the parking lot reminded me of the death of any chance of getting back together with Scott as I'd hoped. A part of me still loved him. Another part of me just wanted revenge. If I was being truthful with myself, I had slept with Aaron to get even with Scott. Now, in the sober light of day, I regretted it. I couldn't believe getting even could feel so awful.

Halloween was two days away—a holiday of the biggest free-for-all of the year at Chico State. But one thing had changed after that drunken night of revenge sex. I'd begun to pray. Really pray. Often and heartfelt pleas for God to help me. I'd spent the past several Sundays alone in church, standing with my head bowed, blinking back tears under stained-glass light. I felt so broken.

A brokenness that wouldn't go away.

As I drove the short distance across town, I asked God to give me a sign.

"If you want me to talk to Scott, please let me hear our song, "Stand by Me," before I get out of this car." Two songs played on the radio as I crossed town, but neither was "Stand by Me." By the time I parked in my space at the apartment complex, I was weeping.

I guess this means it's really over. I walked up the stairs wiping tears from my cheeks. When I opened our apartment door, the song "Stand by Me" hit me in the face. My roommate was watching the movie, and the theme song was playing.

My heart stopped and then pounded madly. I went to my room, closed the door, and cried my eyes out. Partly because I'd gotten the answer I'd hoped for, and partly because God had freaked me out.

An hour later, my roommate knocked on my door and invited me to go out with her to a bar. She was several years older than I was, but I still had my fake ID just a few months shy of my twentieth birthday. At the bar, we had a few drinks, but all I wanted to do was drive to Reno and see Scott.

When I got home that night, I tried to go to bed, but my other roommate had left a note on the bathroom mirror.

"He called again. *PLEASE* call him back!"

It was two a.m. and a drive over the Sierras to the University of Nevada, Reno, was four hours. Half drunk, I got into my car and headed for the Feather River Canyon—the fastest route to Reno.

The further into the mountains I drove, the colder it got in my car. I had left Chico wearing jeans and a short-sleeve T-shirt. Now, I blasted the heater and sobered up fast.

What are you doing? This is insane! You're so stupid. He probably just wants to tell you what a lowlife you are for sleeping with Aaron. Turn around. Turn around. Turn around!

By then, I was almost through the mountains. Dawn was breaking across the desert beyond The Biggest Little City in the World aglow in neon lights.

I knew Scott lived in a couple's converted garage he rented for cheap close to the university. So cheap, I later found out they didn't run the heat for him. It was freezing when I stepped out of my car. My knees shook as I walked to his door.

He probably hates you. You're such a fool. I knocked on the door softly with that mocking voice in my ear. *You've always been a fool for him.*

Prior to this, a year before he broke up with me, I had told him, "You're a bigger sinner than me."

He'd been a good athlete in high school but also smoked pot and drank and slept around. I was a "good girl" in high school. Good grades. Good behavior. I'd earned the Bank of America Award in English my senior year. Sometimes Scott would tease me because I was an eighteen-year-old virgin and had a midnight curfew. He thought my parents and everybody else way too protective of me.

"You're such a little farm girl raised under a butte rock," he'd joke, due to me growing up in the Sutter Buttes. "Everybody shelters you. You don't know a thing. I've never met a girl like you before."

What would he say now when he opened the door? The little farm girl was gone. I'd done so much without him—lost my way so completely. It was Friday morning and I was missing my college classes. Missing Chico's Indian summer in the Sacramento Valley, rubbing my arms up and down to warm them with the high desert cold slipping inside me—all the way inside—as I knocked and knocked and knocked.

Where was he?

Chapter Eight

Sometimes when things are falling apart,
they may actually be falling into place.

— Unknown

He's with another girl…. Of course, he is, you idiot! You drove all the way here when he doesn't want to get back together. The phone calls were to tell you what a slut you are for sleeping with Aaron. Do the walk of shame back to your car! Do the walk of shame for the rest of your life!

Shame. Shame. Shame. It washed over me in waves that stained my cheeks crimson as I strode back to my car.

I couldn't even cry. The tears froze inside me. I felt so alone. So deeply and completely alone as dawn bled the Reno sky red. That little fawn all alone because a man had touched her.

If my dad could only see me now. Had he not taught me anything? It was always "You have to be tough. I've got to put some bark on you. You don't need no one. You just need to be strong." Then, out would slide Dad's belt. "Don't you cry," Dad would warn me before a whupping.

By the time I hit seven, I'd made a vow to die before I'd cry when Dad spanked me.

He spanked me a lot.

To make me tough, he insisted.

Why was I thinking about my dad?

Actually, I was thinking about the day I brought Scott home to meet my parents for the first time. Mom and Dad had gone out for the evening, so we waited for them. I'd fixed dinner, and we'd washed the dishes together. The month before I met Scott, I wrote a little note:

"Please Lord, bring my future husband to me. I want to meet him before I graduate high school."

I stuck the note in my Bible—the Bible I never opened except at Lent each year. I'd get all frustrated long before Easter trying to read it because I didn't understand the Bible and didn't like the way God expected women to obey their husbands. That outraged me. God was a chauvinist. And in the Old Testament, where I usually started reading, he killed people with fire from heaven. I considered myself a liberated woman. What I was liberated from I didn't know, but I wasn't about to obey a man or a god that burned people up.

My thoughts rambled as I sat in my car with my teeth chattering on a hill above the university. I remembered that first night I brought Scott home to the farm. How I took him for a ride on our three-wheeler motorcycle over the green hills of an ancient volcano and down to the flat pasture where Dad grew oat hay for our cattle. Sitting behind me, Scott breathed in my ear, "Slow down, girl." That's all he said in his seductive voice. But, later, once we'd been dating for a while, he told me he thought I would kill us driving so fast in that pasture. He was a freshman in college, the strong, silent type and so beautiful he took my breath away.

Finally, that first night with Scott on the farm, my dad's Toyota Supra drove up the hill and parked in the carport connected to my parents' two-story ranch house. The back-porch screen door banged, and then the laundry room door as Mom walked into the kitchen. She glanced at Scott but seemed distracted. I quickly introduced them, and Scott shook my mom's hand.

"Where's Dad?" I looked behind my mom, waiting to hear the screen door slam again. Sometimes Dad grabbed a beer out of the fridge in the garage. Maybe he was out there getting his brewski.

"Your dad's in jail." Mom walked past us to the kitchen sink to get a drink of water.

I knew she hadn't had any alcohol at the party—Mom wasn't the drinker in the family.

I laughed. Surely, she was joking. "Really, where's Dad?" I was so nervous about him meeting Scott.

"He's in jail. I thought he was going to kill us driving 120 miles an hour on Township Road, when the sheriff pulled us over."

I looked at Scott, and he was watching me. The relaxed, confident expression didn't change on his face. He just stood there, his strong, silent presence comforting me.

"Did Dad get a DUI?"

No response from my mom. Just a gulp of water, and that was it. She went to bed.

For years, I'd expected this. Dad and his friends thought nothing of sliding behind the wheel after drinking up a storm. I grew up riding around with drunk drivers. One of my recurring nightmares happened in a pickup truck. The pickup was going really fast, and I couldn't make it stop. I didn't know the man driving, but he was like a machine, unresponsive to anything I said or did. I knew we'd crash. It was just a matter of time, but I didn't know when or how it would happen. That was the really terrible part—not knowing when the crash would come. Just waiting with everything out of control.

Now, I was standing in the kitchen not knowing when Dad would meet Scott. I'd hoped he would come home sober enough that this first meeting would go well. But it went nowhere. My dad was in jail.

To Scott's credit, he acted like jail was no big deal. "I'll meet him next weekend," he said quietly after my mom left. Then he pulled me into his arms and held me tight. Tears burned my eyes, but I did everything I could to blink them away. I didn't want Scott to see how upset I was.

"We can watch a movie," I said a little too brightly.

"Sounds good."

He tucked a strand of hair behind my ear, his eyes searching mine for a moment that felt far too intimate—like a kiss without clothes. I turned off all the lights and we settled down, side by side on the rug, perched on our elbows watching a Rocky movie. No talking about my dad being arrested.

We never talked about it again.

Just two months later, Scott moved in with us because of a flood. It rained the day we started dating and pretty much poured every day for the rest of the winter. By late February, the three rivers that converge in our valley were raging. A levee broke, and one of those rivers flooded Scott's college town.

My high school friend, Cherie, who worked at J.C. Penney's at the mall was helicoptered off the roof as a wall of water hit the store. Scott arrived on our doorstep with not much more than the clothes on his back the night the levee crumbled just a few miles from his apartment.

My mom was a nurse, and the hospital filled up with wet, traumatized people. She worked overtime. My dad was a civil engineer, and his expertise was needed in a city surrounded by floodwaters.

All the schools closed due to the raging rivers. This left Scott and me alone at my parents' house on the hill with no neighbors in sight for nearly a month without anyone else there during the day.

What were my parents thinking?

For us it was like a honeymoon. A hundred acres in the Sutter Buttes all to ourselves. We rode horses and had picnics in the sunshine when it quit raining. Wildflowers appeared overnight. Spring sprung with a vengeance. The grass was soft and green as Ireland beneath our backs. Side by side, we looked up at the sky and talked for hours. We showed each other our scars and told the stories behind them. For young people, we both had a lot of wounds. Barbed wire had ripped my shoulder open when I was a little girl running from one of Dad's big, mean bulls. Scott had an ugly scar on his back where his mom's boyfriend had run over him with a ski boat in Okinawa, Japan. His Air Force dad was stationed there when Scott was young. His mom was having an affair with another soldier. His dad discovered the boyfriend because Scott landed at the hospital for a whole lot of stitches. This led to an ugly divorce.

I had a long white scar on my wrist I'd gotten while playing hide and seek with Dad when he was drinking. When I was small, we had a lot of parties at our house. Dad shoved me down to hide against the side of the house with kids, dogs, and drunk men running around in the dark. A metal ant poisoning stake at the base of the house slit my wrist open. Dad told me to keep quiet until he felt my warm blood on him. He carried me into the house and sat me on top of the washing machine where my mom doctored me up. Seeing all that blood on Dad and me was horrifying. My parents put my skinny little wrist in a homemade splint because it was after midnight and Mom was too embarrassed to take me to the hospital where she worked. She'd taped butterflies on my injury and Dad fashioned a cast for me out of one of his cardboard tubes that he kept house plans in for his engineering projects.

Monday at school, the kids made fun of my homemade cast. That hurt more than my wound that healed badly. When people saw the long, white scar on my wrist they asked if I'd tried to commit suicide. The scar ran along my blue vein that you could see under my lily-white skin. I was embarrassed about this scar, and the whiteness of my skin, the blue of my veins. Maybe because the scar came with humiliation at school that I hid it from people. *They don't have enough money for a real cast, so hers is cardboard.* That wasn't the reality, but somewhere in my mind, it became my reality. Both Scott and I had scars that had hurt us in more ways than just the physical. I felt so close to him after we shared our scars.

We made out to slow '70s songs on my bedroom floor. I wasn't about to lie on the bed with him yet. He tried to feel me up and I wouldn't let him lift my shirt. Not just because of my breasts, but because of my bellybutton. I had an outie. I showed no one my ugly outie. I hated it. But Scott sensed my angst that night. "Are you hiding another scar?" he asked as he kissed me. I shook my head "no."

"Come on. Remember we promised to always be honest with each other." He kept on kissing me.

His kisses made me tremble. Taking a deep breath, I lifted up my flannel shirt just enough for him to see my outie.

His lips left mine and he took a look. "That's what you're hiding? A cute little outie?" He grinned and leaned down and kissed my belly button. It was the most intimate moment I'd ever experienced at eighteen years old.

"It's ugly," I said, a lump in my throat. I was opening my heart to him. It was terrifying and exhilarating at the same time.

"Babe," he whispered. "There is nothing ugly about you." From then on, we called each other babe.

The music played on, my stereo spinning a spell of young love in my girlhood bedroom. We both favored '70s music over the '80s bands of our time—just born a decade too late, I guess. Meatloaf's "Two Out of Three Ain't Bad" got stuck in my head. Perhaps it bred the lie in both of us that he didn't truly love me. That song lyric became my truth for decades.

I didn't lose my virginity during the flood—a minor miracle— but my heart was long gone. I would have married Scott in the middle of receding floodwaters had he asked me. I was still in high school but didn't care. I would've followed him to hell and back, I loved him that much.

A few months later, it felt like I did.

He'll never know you did this drive of shame if you just drive away now. Just drive home to California and don't look back—Reno in your rearview mirror. Just get out of here fast.

But for some bizarre reason, that tight hug the night my dad was in jail rose in my memory like the floodwaters that washed us into our passionate love affair. There were so many things about Scott I couldn't forget. Couldn't get over. Couldn't outrun.

I wrote a note for him in my car and walked it back to his door, tucking the folded paper in the crack above the lock as I shivered in the cold.

"I drove up to see you, but you're not home. It's for the best. We need to let each other go. Stop calling me!"

At the station on my way out of town, I filled my car with gas and bought a soda and caffeine pills before driving back into the mountains with the heater blasting my face. I'd never taken stimulants, and within an hour of popping several of the tiny caffeine pills, I thought I might throw up. It was a long drive home.

It was only noon when I pulled into my apartment complex thinking I should go to class. I still had two English courses I could make. But I was so sick and sleep-deprived, I decided to retreat to my bed.

Kids were already walking around in costumes in Chico with Halloween the next day. My friend Dana and I had planned to dress up like green leprechauns and go to a big frat party. We'd even bought fake pointed ears and painted them green to go with our Goodwill green clothes. Both of my roommates were sitting in chairs rocking like worried old women when I finally walked through the door.

One was my cousin; the other was like a cousin since we'd grown up together. I couldn't ask for better girls to live with, but Kathy and Kim were livid that I drove to Reno in the middle of the night. It didn't matter they'd found the note I left on the bathroom mirror: "I'm going to see him. Don't worry, I'll be fine."

"Thank God you're alive!" my cousin Kathy said, and I could tell she was really mad.

Both roommates had missed their classes that morning due to staying home waiting for me. After chewing me out, Kathy said, "He called. He was at ROTC PT this morning. You're so dumb."

I didn't even know what PT was. "Physical training," Kathy informed me. "Monday through Friday he works out with the other cadets. That's why he wasn't home—he was out exercising, you fool."

"I'm so glad he wasn't home," I said, on the verge of tears. "That was the stupidest thing I've ever done. I'm sorry."

I walked past them, desperately longing for my bed.

"He'll be here tonight. As soon as he gets out of class, he's hitting the road. You better get some sleep. You look awful," said my cousin. Then Kathy's anger dissolved, and she grinned at me. "I told him to bring a Halloween costume."

"I still love you," Scott said on Halloween, just after midnight, his face painted camo. I stood there staring at him with my mouth hanging open.

Did he really just say that?

It was kind of hard to hear with my green plastic ears on. Only once did he say he loved me when we were dating. It was when he was breaking up with me that last time, and even though his blue eyes were bright with unshed tears, I didn't believe him.

We were walking home from a party, just the two of us, since we'd ditched our group of friends. We had been drinking but were sober enough to talk seriously. He asked me to tell him every detail I could remember about the night with Aaron. Because I had been really drunk, I didn't remember all that well. Maybe I didn't want to recall the revenge sex that ripped my heart out. I cried as we talked. He wasn't wearing a costume, but his face was painted. He was in jeans and a T-shirt with his very short hair—ROTC hair. I was dressed all in green, and it seemed ridiculous to have the gut-wrenching conversation while dressed as a leprechaun.

The houses we passed on the way to my apartment were small cottages with tidy lawns and tall trees shading the sidewalk from the streetlights, making the dark darker. Old peoples' houses all silent and sleeping in a town rocking with wild college parties.

This was vintage Chico.

In the distance, music from a row of fraternity houses drifted on the air. The faint smell of wood smoke lingered. We made it home, still talking about the last nine months apart, mostly the bad things we'd done without each other. I took off my costume ears, wishing the real ones could come off with them. This conversation was so hard.

Scott went into the bathroom and washed the paint off his face while I put on pajamas—pink flannel ones that covered me from neck to toes, including footies, I'm embarrassed to tell you. Wearing little-kid pajamas was my way of saying, "I don't want to grow up yet." They also kept me warm in an apartment where we didn't run the heat in order to keep our utility bill low.

Scott and I talked some more, then he drifted off to sleep on the couch. Alone in my bed, I replayed the night in my head.

Agonizing over it.

Chapter Nine

> You can't go back and change the beginning,
> but you can start where you are
> and change the ending.
>
> — C.S. Lewis

By Halloween morning Scott was gone. I fretted while he spent the day with his brother Rick, who was also attending college in Chico, but Scott returned that evening to attend a party with some friends and me. I dressed in a short leather skirt I'd borrowed from my roommate's sexy friend. It was royal blue, soft and pliable, and fit me like Saran Wrap.

Halloween night in Chico is known for being out of control. Scott and I drank beer and ate brownies at a frat party.

"They're crunchy," I said, somewhat surprised by the brownies' texture. Obviously, frat boys didn't know how to make brownies.

"Don't eat anymore." Scott studied his half-eaten brownie. "I think they're laced with marijuana."

Why was this so shocking to me? I'd already eaten a brownie.

"I'm ready to go home," I announced, completely fed up with *Playboy*'s top party town.

It was Saturday night, and I suddenly longed for church in the morning. I was so tired of parties. Tired of the drinking. Tired of people messing up good old-fashioned brownies, something I'd never even heard of before.

"Okay, let's go," he said.

Taking my hand, we walked into the night, into the cold Chico air, but the air didn't cool my face. The world began to spin. I had no idea which way to get to my apartment. Scott was feeling the brownies too.

An hour later, having walked in circles, we found ourselves sprawled side by side on some old person's lawn—one of those nice little cottage yards. I'd never felt so out of it in my life. Scott was still holding my hand.

"I'm in the military now. I can't be doing drugs," he said.

"I want to go home," I told him again, on the verge of tears.

"We'll find your apartment. Let's just lie here for a while and sober up."

"I don't want to go home to my apartment. I want to go home to the farm." I was sick to death of drugs, alcohol, and college life.

"Then let's go home to the farm." Scott rolled over and kissed me.

I was freezing in my short blue leather skirt. His warm lips felt so good. I snuggled close to him as he wrapped his arms around me, and we kissed as if we were alone in a bedroom, not lost on a senior citizen's lawn. This was not lust. This was *I really missed you*. It could have been an airport reunion or a roll in the surf like in *From Here to Eternity,* that 1950s film that was so risqué for its time. Our kiss was so good, it was painful.

After we finally lifted ourselves off the grass, we reached my apartment, and Scott carried me into my bedroom where we reclaimed everything I thought we had lost. We broke my bed along with the barriers between us. Later, after sleeping until noon in my broken bed frame, wrapped around each other like seahorses, we drove home to the farm.

It was Sunday. The golden grass of autumn greeted us in the Sutter Buttes where Dad's cattle grazed in the waning afternoon light. A soft, crisp breeze rustled the oak trees, promising an early winter. We rolled down the windows to the cry of a red-tailed hawk as we passed the barn. I shivered with pleasure. We were almost home.

"Let's drive to Reno and get married right now," Scott said without offering a ring or taking a knee. Without anything but a long, slow kiss that left me trembling on the first day of November.

All Saints' Day.

"Let's just be engaged for now," I responded with a teary smile. I wasn't ready to marry. My broken heart hadn't healed, but I was willing to take all our brokenness and give it another try.

For the next year and a half, we were engaged. And I found that Scott's heart was as damaged as mine.

"I never slept with one of your friends," he told me one night (as we carried on a long-distance relationship from different colleges). He sounded so sincere, so injured, as he said it.

"You slept with, like, fifty girls. I only slept with one other person in my whole life." I grew hurt and angry over the phone.

"Yeah, but it was Aaron. I keep imagining you two together. It's tearing me up."

I heard the pain in his voice.

My revenge felt complete—bitter but complete. I never knew I had the balls to really hurt Scott. I never believed he really loved me, so how could I wound him so deeply? I told myself he had reaped the night I spent with Aaron. He had sown the soil of infidelity first.

Yet, deep down, in some mystical way, I knew Scott had become like Christ for me. He'd loved me at my darkest. Forgiven my worst deed. Me, the woman who had wept over Christ's feet, washing them with her tears, drying the skin of God with her harlot's hair. Deep down I felt like a whore.

The following weekend, when we met up, he pushed my long auburn hair away from my face. "I want to see your eyes," he said as our bodies joined. His skin so tan, mine white as milk against his brown flesh.

"Look at me," he insisted as we made love. "I need you to see me not Aaron."

Chapter Ten

> It takes courage to grow up and
> become who you really are.
>
> — E.E. Cummings

Sometimes I would open my eyes when he asked me to—to look at him as we were making love. But other times I wouldn't. I told Scott if he ever threw Aaron in my face again, I would make a list of all the girls he'd poked.

"What is poked?" he asked, the look on his face priceless.

"Haven't you read *Lonesome Dove*? It won the Pulitzer Prize!"

"I don't read unless I have to."

"Well, Gus poked a lot of women in that story."

"You mean had sex with them?"

"Duh!"

He got my point.

For months on the weekends when we were able to see each other, we looked at each other deeply, searching each other's souls. He was committed. I was confused. Our roles had reversed. I was the one wanting freedom now. I didn't sleep with anyone else, had no desire to at all, but I partied with my friends and flirted with other guys. I dreamed of moving to San Francisco to become like Danielle Steel, my favorite best-selling author with her seven kids. Yet, I wasn't sure about having babies with Scott. I didn't even know if I would really marry him.

I didn't trust us.

Our relationship was like a cliff. Either of us could jump off at any moment. He no longer partied while becoming a soldier, going to the Army's jump school in Georgia, learning how to use a parachute. He was growing up.

I was free-falling.

Six months after becoming engaged, we moved in together in Reno with two other ROTC cadets. It was a condo in which we had the upstairs to ourselves and the other two guys had the downstairs. I was still not sure I wanted to get married, though I woke up each morning relieved to be in bed with Scott again. Perhaps that's why I was with him. I couldn't imagine waking up to someone else's face beside me on the pillow. But marriage terrified me. My parents were on the verge of killing each other in California.

My dad was out of control in a midlife crisis. My mom was trying to beat some sense into him with a frying pan—literally. He had bruises from her kitchenware.

Six more months into our engagement, my parents called one night. I was in my flannel footie pajamas doing homework—endless English papers I actually enjoyed writing.

"We need you to come home," my parents said in unison over the phone. This was back when there were no cell phones. Homes had phones in different rooms attached to the wall. My parents were in separate parts of the house, talking on the same line with me.

When I drove home in my pajamas, arriving at the ranch house around midnight after honking at the cows to get them out of the road, my parents greeted me at the back door in the laundry room. They'd had another fight.

I couldn't believe how bruised and shattered they both looked.

"Let's all just get some sleep," I said after hugging them tight. "Things will be better in the morning."

But early the next morning, two shotgun blasts woke me from a deep sleep. I fell out of bed, shocked and sick on the floor.

They'd gone and done it.

I stumbled down the stairs unable to breathe. It was dead still and absolutely quiet. I stood at their bedroom door for an endless moment.

A shotgun isn't pretty. Blood will be everywhere. Please, God, please, please, please, no. My legs shook so badly I could hardly walk into their room. I opened the door and made my way down the hall between their bathroom and bedroom, passing the wall of family photos. Then gazed all around. Brown carpet still brown. White walls still white. Their bedsheets were tangled but clean. No one was in the bed or the bedroom. Dawn was breaking with sunlight streaming through the bedroom windows. The sliding glass door stood ajar.

At least they did it outside. *I can just hose their blood off the patio.*

I wasn't thinking clearly. A part of me was so mad at them.

I didn't see any blood on the concrete when I stepped outside. Finally, I spotted Dad standing on the porch in his whitey tightie underwear, shotgun in hand. His skinny white legs looked like a chicken's shoved into his cowboy boots. I doubted he was wearing socks.

"Where's Mom?" Suspicion laced my voice.

"She got called in to work a few hours ago." Dad looked around, still hunting.

I surveyed the rolling hills covered with oak trees. Cattle grazed down in the pasture, horses in the distance, their tails swishing in the early morning light. The country of my childhood was so beautiful. "What did you just shoot?" I still wasn't completely convinced it wasn't my mom he unloaded a round on.

"A woodpecker. There's another one around here somewhere. They're tearing up the house." He let out a string of cuss words, looking around for the birds.

"It's six o'clock in the morning." Relief rioted through me before I got even madder. "Woodpeckers? Really, Dad?" My parents were driving me off the deep end.

"Why are you up so early?" Dad asked.

"I thought you killed each other."

Dad laughed. "I won't kill your mom, but she might kill me."

"This isn't funny!"

With Dad standing there in his underwear and cowboy boots holding his shotgun, it really would have been funny if I hadn't been so angry.

"Go back to bed," Dad said with affection in his eyes.

"I've got school this morning!" I suddenly yelled. "Why am I your peacemaker? Get yourselves a counselor. Or lawyer. I'm so done with your insanity!"

Stomping back into the house, I retrieved my purse from my room with a change of clothes still in my car. I didn't even bother to brush my teeth. Still in my pajamas, I jumped behind the wheel and sped back to Reno.

I pondered during the three-hour drive over the mountains. Why on earth would I want to get married and end up like my lunatic parents?

My mom worked all the time at the hospital. She was a great nurse. It was how she coped with Dad in his midlife crisis—by making her nursing career her whole world, with the exception of her rose garden that she tended in the still of the evening when her husband was out hound-dogging around.

In her mid-forties, struggling with arthritis, she still had a trim figure and pretty face. The last thing I wanted was to end up like my poor mom—because all men cheat.

So, why get married?

Why put myself through this misery?

When I got home from work that night, I tried to explain to Scott why I didn't want to get married. Angst over my parents was wrecking me.

"Marriage scares the daylights out of me," I told him.

"Marry me or move out," he said. I saw in his eyes how serious he was. I couldn't believe it. I felt like throwing up.

I was so tired after driving over the mountains at daybreak, going to school, then on to my shift at a Catholic day care run by nuns. Afterward, to my second job as a cocktail waitress at a nearby casino. My two jobs seemed nearly the same—everybody was thirsty, and they all wanted their drinks and snacks *now*.

It was late. I hadn't had much sleep. The last thing I wanted to do was get married after watching my mom and dad act out *War of the Roses*.

But Scott was standing there in his ROTC uniform waiting for my response. When did he become such a man? I was so afraid to become a woman.

Men treated women badly.

I went and packed a bag and walked out onto the condo's snow-covered porch. It was February and freezing outside. If I broke my engagement, I'd be leaving Reno. This was not a town I wanted to live in single again.

I stood there for a while in six inches of snow, my feet freezing. My heart aching. My soul waking to the reality that I could take a chance on love or turn my back and run away. I stared at the snow and grew even colder. Finally, I lugged my bag back inside, tucked it away in the closet, and climbed into bed with Scott.

"So ... you'll marry me?" he whispered in the dark, pulling me close and nuzzling my neck.

I pressed my face against his warm chest and whispered, "Yes."

Then I cried myself to sleep in his arms.

The next morning, I awoke to an empty bed.

Scott left before dawn every weekday morning to do ROTC physical training. I didn't see him all day until after my job at the day care. It was Tuesday, the night I had off from the casino, so we could attend our Beer & Wine Tasting class together—a surprisingly hard college course. Endless memorizing of wine regions, the cultivation of vines, the chemistry of grapes, the whole wine-making process. All this before we got to taste at the end of class. We signed up for it to culture ourselves, to give up college beer parties and learn to appreciate wine. But I studied more for this course than all my English classes put together. I wasn't about to let a beer-and-wine-tasting class ruin my GPA.

"Wear something nice, so we can head to the chapel after class," Scott said as I shoveled food in my mouth standing in our condo's small kitchen. Full-time school and two part-time jobs left little time for preparing meals. It hit me. He was dead serious. I couldn't swallow the carrots I was chewing.

He really is going to make me marry him or move out.

Speechless, I left the kitchen and headed for my closet upstairs in our bedroom, not sure if I would take the bag I'd already packed and just leave or get dressed up like he said I should. In my walk-in closet, I slid a cassette tape of Bette Midler's "The Rose" into my recorder. Listening to music always calmed me down. Grandma Helen made me tapes of the song lists I sent to her in California.

I listened to Bette's famous ballad and cried while changing my clothes.

I could move back to the farm and fall out of bed in the morning when Dad shot woodpeckers in his underwear, or I could get married.

Should I stay or should I go?

Marriage was such a risk.

We'd been engaged a little over a year. We worked, went to school, and would rather go out to a quiet dinner alone than to a party with our friends. I realized Scott had become my best friend. He was my favorite human being in the whole world. I wasn't ready to marry him, but I sure didn't want to lose him. I'd done my best to forget how he broke my heart with those other girls. How I broke his heart by getting revenge with Aaron.

Standing in my closet as Bette sang on, I slipped into a pink blouse, white fitted skirt, and high-heeled pumps. The best clothes I owned.

I'd rather dress up than break up.

At the end of class, I tasted more wine than usual because I was drinking for courage. Then, we drove to Chapel of the Bells in downtown Reno.

I was glad I didn't blink standing there in front of a man dressed like Elvis. I would have missed my own wedding. It was over that fast.

A Chapel of the Bells employee drove us to the courthouse at ten p.m. that night to sign our marriage certificate. Afterward, we bought a bottle of cheap champagne at Safeway. I was barely twenty-one, my groom just twenty-two. We still watched adolescent movies together, like *Honey I Shrunk the Kids* and Charlie Brown specials.

What in the world had we done?

We drove up the mountain overlooking Reno to make our wedding toast. The ground was covered with fresh snow, and our car—a little Dodge Charger—didn't have a heater or even a reverse gear. Both were broken. After parking on a cliff looking out over the neon lights of the city, we realized we couldn't back up. The irony did not escape me.

After a quick toast to us, my new husband got out of the car and pushed it backward away from the precipice as I steered us safely off the ledge. Saving ourselves would take teamwork for the rest of our lives if we made it that far. I didn't know if we'd make it to tomorrow.

With my new, muddy husband, and me freezing, we returned to the condo to climb into the bathtub together where we drank champagne and laughed about getting the car stuck on the edge of the abyss. The whole thing felt like a dream. I didn't feel married. My feet and hands stung as they warmed up from the cold. I was more concerned about frostbite than our elopement.

The next morning we went off to school like nothing had happened. I continued to work at the day care and casino and study English at the university while Scott finished ROTC, preparing to become an Army helicopter pilot after graduation.

We also moved ahead with planning our big, fat Catholic wedding with nobody but our best friends knowing we'd eloped. My life was out of control, but in a different way than I'd ever experienced before. I was about to become an Army wife.

Our Catholic wedding was set to take place the week Scott graduated from college. By the time it was upon us after his graduation in Nevada, we were hardly speaking to each other. We took separate cars to the farm where everyone was gathering. The night before our wedding ceremony with hundreds of guests in my hometown, I told Scott that I didn't want to go through with it.

I wanted out.

Chapter Eleven

I would rather die of passion than of boredom.
— Vincent Van Gogh

"It's too late. We're already married." The determination on Scott's face matched the grit in his voice.

We had a big fight after the rehearsal dinner, where we ate Mexican food and drank margaritas. Our wedding party, all kids in their early twenties, were wild. Neither of us got drunk like our friends. My soon-to-be spouse, already my Nevada husband, said I should have a drink to kill the bug that was up my butt. Of course, he didn't say "butt." His language was saltier than that as we quarreled in the restaurant's parking lot under a palm tree.

The following day we were barely speaking to each other. We'd spent the night at the farm in separate bedrooms with our bridesmaids and groomsmen. Early that morning, my mom had the wedding party out picking her sweet peas in the garden she had grown for our nuptials. Thousands of sweet peas. Hungover groomsmen carried baskets of the delicate little flowers that smelled so sweet with the groomsmen reeking of alcohol.

Scott sat silently in front of the TV watching Bugs Bunny. I walked past him feeling like a trapped animal in a wedding circus. He reached out and pulled me onto his lap.

"Watch cartoons with me." It was more of a plea than a command.

I settled on his lap. He wrapped his arms around me and held tight as if he was afraid I would run away. I did want to run away. I desperately wanted to run away. Soon, he was laughing at Bugs Bunny while I tried not to cry. Scott always laughed at Bugs Bunny. I'd found it endearing when we were first dating. Now, I thought he was too immature to get married. *Again.*

My mom was bossing everyone around, this was mostly a do-it-yourself, country wedding, but she left Scott alone. "He's the groom," she said, herding his poor groomsmen back out the door to pick roses after the sweet peas. Once I was on Scott's lap, she left me alone too.

That night, during our wedding ceremony, one of the groomsmen got so nervous, he passed out. The poor guy hit the Spanish-styled church's stucco wall, and two other groomsmen helped him stand back up. The priest didn't even slow down. He rolled right on with reciting the vows. When we met with Father O'Leary before the wedding, I told him I did not want to say that I would obey my husband.

Father replied, "I will not marry you unless you say you'll obey."

So, I said the vow, knowing full well I was lying through my teeth. I had no intention of obeying my husband. Like the groomsmen, I would have preferred to pass out and wake up single again. Thunder rolled outside the church and rain pattered on the roof. Our reception was outdoors at the fairgrounds. I worried it would be rained out.

At the wedding reception, the thunderstorm blew over, but it was a cold night for the end of May. People milled around shivering in their summer outfits and drinking a lot. My parents had a terrible argument, and my brother and his roommate ended up in a fistfight on the dance floor because they were plastered. Scott got hammered, too. This wasn't like him at all. I'd never seen him really drunk before.

I had decided I would be a sober bride. One sip of champagne was all I allowed myself during the toast. I was holding myself together come hell or high water. We'd agreed to no cake smashing in the face. Our wedding party was disappointed that we carefully fed each other small pieces, but I could see Scott was already well on his way to feeling no pain.

We made it through our first dance to "Stand by Me," and later Scott was shaking it up on the dancefloor with his best man Rick, and his other brothers Victor and Miguel. After the divorce, Scott's dad had remarried Emma from the Dominican Republic. Scott had a handful of siblings in their twenties and boy, could they dance. All of Scott's family oozed rhythm. My white-as-Wonder Bread, small-town relatives waltzed, square danced, and the chicken dance was a safe, fun bet, but rhythm had all but escaped us.

I was standing beside my great-aunt, Rose, Grandma Anne's older sister and my very Catholic godmother, when the bass began thumping and Scott and his brothers began bumping. His groomsmen joined in the show. Scott's big city, multicultural posse was taking over the dancefloor, Scott right in the middle cutting loose. My husband can really dance when he wants to. I longed to cover Aunt Rose's eyes. They about fell out of her head when she saw my groom—Elvis the pelvis—with his brothers reenacting a Chippendales show. Tuxedo jackets went flying. Thank God they kept the rest of their clothes on. Aunt Rose and her husband Elwood quickly left the reception. So did my grandparents. All the older people skedaddled out of there in a hurry.

I wanted to disappear. I wanted to hogtie Scott. I white-knuckled it through the rest of the reception. The night only got worse. I ate one strawberry for dinner. I don't remember Scott eating, but I'm sure he did. He's usually the first one in the food line. Pretty soon, he was dancing with a twelve-year-old girl with an eye patch. Actually, he kept sliding away from her as she trailed him around the dance floor like a devoted puppy.

"She won't leave me alone," Scott said when I finally mustered the courage to approach him among the dancers. "Who is that girl?" he asked, dragging me into his arms, holding a beer bottle in one hand and spilling some of it down my back.

I clenched my teeth as the cold beer splashed down my spine. "I've babysat that girl since she was born. She's a neat kid. Be nice to her."

"She's annoying the hell out of me. Why aren't you dancing with me? You've been hiding. I thought you left me."

"You're out of control." I tried to keep my voice low. "Stop drinking."

"Can we leave now?"

"No, it's too early."

"It's not too early for me. Let's start the honeymoon right now." Scott grabbed my behind in both hands, a drunken grin on his face as he tried to kiss me.

"My parents are here! All their friends are watching. Get your hands off my butt."

"We're married. Double married. Damn your dress is big. I can't even find your a— in all this satin. What a big a— dress…

I wrestled out of his arms. "I need to greet people. My cousins drove a long way for us tonight."

"You have a hundred cousins. I don't even know these people. I don't care about them. Dance with me." Scott stumbled while trying to capture me in his arms again. "Save me from the girl with the eye patch," he pleaded.

"Save yourself," I tossed over my shoulder as I hurried away and the girl with the eye patch bounced right back over.

I went and visited with a middle-aged couple I'd never met before. After a good half hour, them laughing and pounding down their drinks and complimenting me on my red hair and a great reception, I finally found the courage to ask, "So, how do I know you?"

Scott had grown up mostly on the East Coast. I knew they weren't his guests. "Are you my cousins?" I asked.

"Oh, no, we're from across the fairgrounds at another wedding reception. It's really boring over there." They lowered their voices like I was in cahoots with them. "It's a dry wedding. Can you believe that?" The husband asked, "Where's your drink, honey? Do you want me to grab you a beer or do you prefer wine?"

"Maybe she wants whiskey," the wife said. "I like bourbon and Coke." She held up her red cup. Only wine and beer were available at the bar. I had no idea where she got the hard stuff, though I saw bottles floating around, snuck in by rowdy guests.

My throat was sore from talking with people. The weeks leading up to this wedding had been exhausting with finishing our college classes, completing our final days at our jobs, and entertaining Scott's family, who came out two weeks early to explore California.

"Well, thanks for joining us tonight. Glad you're having fun." I walked away from that couple feeling like I'd had it up to my eyeballs. I didn't care that the DJ was now spinning '80s music, which I hated. I was so done with this wild bash. Scott had finally given up trying to escape the eye-patch girl on the dancefloor. He was over with one of his groomsmen now, our college roommate, Fred, Scott's best friend from ROTC. Was that a tequila bottle Fred was feeding Scott the way you bottle feed a calf?

"I'm taking care of my man," Fred said as he tucked his tequila away when I marched up to them. "Scott wants to go home. He's ready for the honeymoon," Fred patted Scott on the back as if comforting him. Both Scott and I loved Fred. He was the most loyal friend we had, but I wanted to snatch that tequila bottle from him and hit them both on the head with it. Maybe hit myself too. To put me out of my misery.

"There's my... little... wifey." Scott reached out, trying to get a hold of my "big a— dress" as he'd called it earlier. That had hurt my feelings. I dodged his grasp. His white tuxedo pants were covered in grass stains and black skid marks. I'd seen him wrestling with his groomsmen earlier over by the bathrooms on the fairground lawns. His shirt was ripped. I had no idea where his jacket had landed. All my bridesmaids were wearing the groomsmen's jackets because the night had grown so cold. My best friend, Christy, and her husband, Jason, were set to drive us to our bed and breakfast. I was so relieved when they walked over.

"Ready to go?" Christy asked with a sweet smile on her face, her little dimples showing. My sober matron of honor had arrived to rescue me. Praise the Lord. Fred and Jason helped get Scott to the car. Christy and I trailed behind, her trying to make me feel better. We'd been best friends since we were twelve years old. I didn't even have to say anything. Christy knew how upset I was.

Scott crawled into the front seat with Jason, while Christy and I slid into the backseat together.

"I want Carl's Jr.," Scott started in before we even got out of the parking lot. "I need a Double Bacon Western Cheeseburger with guacamole." He slurred his words in the passenger seat.

"Absolutely not," I cried. "How trashy is that? I'm not going to Carl's Jr. in my wedding dress! High-schoolers hang out at Carl's Jr., for crying out loud."

Scott kept on begging for Carl's Jr. as we hit the highway heading south. At least he wasn't a mean drunk. He sounded like a little boy nobody had fed in a week. "I'm hungry," he kept saying.

"There was a ton of food at the reception," I said tightly. "I'm sure you ate your fill."

"That was hours ago. I need food." Scott draped himself over the back seat to talk to me. He reeked of alcohol. "Come on wifey…"

"Stop calling me that! Get your safety belt on," I commanded.

"I want Carl's Jr.," he pleaded.

I want to kill you. I was thinking. I gave up on speaking to him. When I clammed up, Christy whispered in my ear, "We'll go through the drive-thru. Just let him get his burger. It will be better in the morning."

Christy was in her second year of marriage already. I trusted her judgment. I slid way down in my seat, trying to hide in the drive-thru in a big, fat, puffy white wedding dress with shoulder sleeves the size of cannon balls. It was 1989 after all; everything was big in the '80s, including my red hair. In the morning I would seek a divorce. *Two* divorces—since I was now legally married in both Nevada and California.

At our bed and breakfast suite in an old Victorian house near the river, Scott made love to his Double Bacon Western Cheeseburger instead of me. Guacamole was spread across the sheets.

I slept in a wingback chair. It was a very uncomfortable night. Strangely enough, the honeymoon went surprisingly well. Our chemistry was astounding, and Scott could make me laugh, even when I was mad at him. We stayed in fancy bed and breakfasts on the coast and looked at happy seals on our honeymoon in Half Moon Bay and San Francisco. The winding California coastline was so scenic and surprisingly quiet that Memorial Day weekend. We stopped at a lighthouse, kissed on the cliffs, and watched a couple of brave surfers take on the Mavericks. The following year, 1990, the rest of the world would discover this big wave surfing destination too, but for now, it was just us and a couple of skinny guys in worn-out wetsuits giving the Mavericks a go.

It was our first real vacation together.

A year and a half later, I was a young mother to a precious baby girl born in "Sweet Home Alabama," the place Scott learned to fly helicopters for the Army.

We moved across the United States and on to Europe, where I learned to drive a hundred miles an hour on the autobahn with my baby in the backseat. Going eighty was going slow in Germany. The Berlin Wall had just come down, and we had a piece of it on a bookshelf in our living room in Nuremburg. But I hadn't stopped building that wall around my heart. I knew I would need it when my husband cheated on me because, you know it: all men cheat. The only question was when.

Chapter Twelve

I keep a close watch on this heart of mine ....
— Johnny Cash

In the beginning, my marriage was all highs and lows. I flew home from Germany with a one-year-old baby girl on my hip, hoping to find my balance on the farm. Life as a military wife was hard. I was home for only a week, when the high school of my cousin Kiley became the first ever in my lifetime where kids were killed in a shooting.

When the shooter walked in, Kiley ran out of the class, and hid in a bathroom while a teacher and several kids died in that classroom. For hours, we didn't know if Kiley was dead or alive. The shooter took a roomful of students hostage, and in those days, the policy was to wait and see—they didn't enter the school to stop the shooter, fearing it would result in more casualties.

The shooter eventually gave himself up without harming his hostages, but that day harmed our family. Especially my uncle Dan, my dad's little brother. Uncle John was the oldest of my dad's three brothers, then came Dad, Dan, and Gene. The brothers weren't close, but Uncle John and Uncle Dan didn't have kids, so they lavished love on me, Patrick, and my cousins Matt and Kiley.

Kiley lost friends in that school shooting.

"They had their whole lives ahead of them," Uncle Dan said when he came to see me at my parents' house, where I was staying during my visit home. "I can't believe those kids are dead."

My uncle had been fighting depression, which was so weird since he was normally the family clown who kept everyone laughing. We talked all afternoon. The whole time Uncle Dan held my one-year-old daughter, Cami, on his lap. They were quite the pair. He adored her, and Cami loved his attention. We laughed a lot but also covered some serious ground.

My uncle reflected on the L.A. riots, along with the high school shooting. How California was going off the rails. He wondered how to fix it.

"I wish I could die in place of those kids at Kiley's school," my uncle said, all laughter gone.

"Kiley's okay," I reassured him.

When Kiley was small, Uncle Dan paid for him to attend Catholic school. Uncle Dan helped raise Kiley and Matt. He also considered me the daughter he never had and loved me dearly. He worried about my future and talked about the past, sharing his memories of how much he'd enjoyed my childhood. He even talked about Jesus as I glanced through the old records he'd brought to the farm. I picked out my favorite one, pointing to a song I loved when I was a little girl: "El Paso" by Marty Robbins.

I didn't notice as my uncle left that he took the Marty Robbins record from its album cover and carried it home with him.

When he arrived back in his own living room, he put the record on his stereo, turned up the volume so he could hear it in the garage, where he had work to do. The note he wrote was short, thoughtful, and to the point.

He ended it with "I've made my peace with Jesus" before signing, *"Love, Danny."*

Then he placed a rope around his neck and hung himself from a rafter in his garage.

The Marty Robbins's record spun on a loop in his living room, repeating itself over and over.

Grandma Helen found her son less than thirty minutes after his death with the record still playing. Must have been her mother's instinct that took her there so quickly. I was the first person she called.

"He's done it," Grandma Helen said in a breathless voice.

Three years after my wedding—the ceremony my uncle had happily videotaped—I sat on freshly mowed grass beside his body. He was covered with a blanket awaiting the morgue's taxi. It was so like my uncle to mow the lawn before killing himself … after spending that summer afternoon with me. For years I couldn't forgive him for leaving me to go home and fashion a noose. For years, I wondered what I could have said, what I could have done, to stop him from dying.

Normally, I'm a crier, but not a tear came forth as I sat with his body on the grass. Not a single tear until I woke the next morning having slept the shock away.

After that I couldn't stop crying.

At his funeral in the foothills where we buried him beside my Grandpa John in a small old cemetery on the side of a hill, I wore a classy dress and high heels. After the graveside service, we went to Uncle John's Victorian. All his gay friends were there. My dad and his friends were there. But I don't remember seeing any of Uncle Dan's friends except the best friend who cut him down from the garage rafter. That best friend couldn't even speak to anyone, he was so upset.

Uncle Dan took us kids to the movies, cut our fingernails, and teased us unmercifully. It never dawned on me that he was socially awkward until his funeral, where most of the people there were his brothers' friends. Dad had been holding on to me since the graveside service, where Grandma Helen insisted we all go forward to look down at Uncle Dan dead in his casket. There he lay in a brand-new suit. Uncle Dan never wore a suit in his life. He lived in cutoff jeans or his grocery store uniform, running Lucky's produce department for as long as I could remember. I used to think he had the most important job in the world. Dad had his own engineering firm, but Uncle Dan ruled a grocery store. I loved watching him stack lettuce heads and lug watermelons around. Out of all my dad's brothers, Uncle Dan was the closest to our family. My dad walked up, blinked into the casket, and then stumbled away, out across the other graves like a man groping in the darkness.

I chased after Dad, wobbling in my heels. When I caught up with him, I anchored my arm through his. We remained that way at the wake.

Dad slugged down his beer while talking with an old friend who wouldn't take his eyes off me.

"I see you've done really well for yourself," said this old friend to Dad.

The man's stare roved up and down my body, his gaze eating me alive. I didn't like men with hungry eyes. I did my best to ignore him.

Dad gripped his beer and my arm and didn't seem to know where the conversation was going. But I knew where it was going, and I was desperately looking around for my mom. She needed to come and stand with Dad, to show this jerk she was still his wife. Clearly, the guy thought I was dad's girlfriend.

"When did you part ways with Carolyn?" the old friend asked as his eyes ravished me.

The only reason I was still standing there was due to Dad's death grip.

"Carolyn?" Dad said, confused.

I knew in his mind he was still back at the casket staring down at his dead brother. I could see he wasn't thinking straight.

"I'm going to get Mom," I told him as I looked into that man's eyes, feeling like a cornered animal—warning him, begging him, hating him. I had met men like him in other places but never at a funeral. It had always been at my waitressing jobs. Or on a plane or in a bar where I was prepared for the passes. My disgust in men multiplied that day.

Why were guys so selfish? So lustful? Such cheaters? This man was married. He'd come to the funeral with his wife. Where the heck was she?

"This is my daughter," Dad said, finally joining the conversation. I pried Dad's arm loose, more than tempted to take his beer and throw it in the man's face. How I wished Scott was with me, but he was off flying Army helicopters as usual. With a pilot husband I was mostly alone in life with our baby girl. Our tiny daughter hadn't managed to stop men from coming on to me. I found this so surprising and disgusting.

Who comes on to a mom with a little baby?

"You have a beautiful daughter," the man said to Dad as I walked away as fast as I could, trying not to lose my balance in heels I wasn't used to wearing.

I ran into my Uncle John on the deck of his Victorian mansion. He took my elbow to steady me. "You okay, honey?"

I wanted to fall into his arms, sobbing. At least gay men didn't treat me like a piece of meat. I felt safe with gay men.

"I'm okay," I said, my voice trembling.

"I just want you to know you've made me proud today," Uncle John said. "I didn't know your kind of class could come from our kind of family. You should dress up more often, honey. You look like a million bucks."

I smiled for him, but the raw grief of losing Uncle Dan left me reeling.

It took years to make peace with his death. And in the end, it wasn't the years that helped me. Jesus helped me. But that came later.

For now, I was alone at funerals. And weddings. And everything else. My husband was off flying for the military. Before I knew it, we had three small children as I began to contemplate ending my marriage. Scott was hardly ever home. I was lonely and unhappy. But did I really have the guts to leave him?

Chapter Thirteen

> We are only as blind as we want to be.
>
> — Maya Angelou

I never really thought my marriage would last, so I wasn't surprised to find myself wanting a divorce a decade into it. We were in Las Vegas for our tenth anniversary, and all I wanted to do was fly home and file the papers. The lights, the casinos, the alcohol left me empty. In our hotel room before we had sex, Scott flipped on a porn station. This had become a routine part of our marriage, and I hated it.

I hated that I was supposed to be a cool wife. Other wives had counseled me about participating in my husband's porn habit, telling me to enjoy it along with him.

"Women can learn to be really sexy from porn," another pilot's wife assured me.

But I didn't feel sexy. I felt used. Like a blow-up doll without a brain. Without a soul. My soul was withering in my marriage.

I felt a million miles away during our lovemaking with a husband who seemed more like a stranger now. I cried after having sex. I missed the kids, especially our one-year-old son I was still nursing. Scott insisted we leave him at home with his grandma. All I wanted to do was to get back to my baby boy, load up his two older sisters, and drive home to the farm.

The farm ... how far away it seemed.

We lived in San Diego, where Scott was serving in the military, flying missions along the border. We'd moved more than a dozen times in ten years. My hair was bleached blond now—I began dying it after our second child was born—and I shopped at Nordstrom's and Macy's for makeup and clothes. Everyone told me how pretty I was. My kids were pretty. My life was pretty. But, really, it wasn't. I'd won a writing contest and landed a big-time New York literary agent who was trying to sell my first real novel, but I'd never been so low in my life. I drank coffee while writing in the morning. Wine as I wrote at night. Scott was rarely around. When he was home, we fought. We were both ambitious, our careers coming first.

On my bathroom counter sat a jewelry box inlaid with Italian wood. When I opened it to pick out my diamond stud earrings, the song "Amazing Grace" played. I quickly closed the lid to avoid hearing that song. It wasn't supposed to be "Amazing Grace." On our honeymoon in San Francisco at a music store, we had picked out that box together—Scott's wedding gift to me. Selecting a special song came with the purchase. I wanted "Stand by Me" or

"The Rose"—the two songs from our wedding. But the store had neither, so we settled on "Amazing Grace."

I found that song stuck in my head day after day. It was so annoying and unnerving. One morning in church, I saw a vision: a life-sized statue of the sacred heart of Jesus began to shine during Mass—a bright white light lasering out of the heart on the statue. Nobody seemed to notice it but me. The heavenly light made me cry. I couldn't stop crying that Sunday. I wept all day long.

But the vision didn't change my life. I chalked it up to something weird. Something unexplainable. A supernatural blip. Instead of trying to figure it out, I just kept going through the motions while each day grew harder.

I attended church regularly but always left feeling frustrated and upset. Scott wouldn't go to Mass with me. Church was a pain in the butt—literally—with the solid wooden pews under my rear end and the kids bouncing up and down beside me. All Mass did was leave me feeling broken because I knew deep down I was a sinner. And busted as a mother too, since my kids wouldn't behave in church. Especially my toddler son, who peed in the church parking lot, ate old gum from under the pews, and broke his sisters' crayons and threw them around, hitting the old lady kneeling in front of us. I was ready to wring Luke's little neck, and I was supposed to confess this to a priest—that I was ready to abuse a child. But ever since my confirmation in the eighth grade, I'd refused to do confession. Who wants to sit in a dark closet with a priest, anyway?

Why was I still torturing myself with church?

"Well, I see the church lady is home," Scott said when I walked through the door after Mass, dragging our little blond son by his collar. Luke was so cute, but I was ready to kill him—and my husband too.

"You should go to church with me just to make your kids behave," I told Scott.

"I don't know why you even bother with church. It puts you in a foul mood and ruins our Sundays."

We had this running argument for years over Sunday mornings. Scott wanted me to lie in bed and have sex with him when he wasn't off flying for the Army somewhere. Instead, I would get up, get the kids dressed, and dutifully go to church. Then, come home frustrated that the kids acted like wild jackrabbits, with old people giving me the stink-eye because of my bad children. And every Sunday I was mad at my husband, who promised before we married that together we would raise our kids Catholic, but he never followed through. If nothing else, I was persistent in making all of us suffer through each crummy Sunday, year after year.

"It's God's day," I said self-righteously. "The kids and I go to church."

"And we all suffer," said Cami, only in the second grade and already hating church.

"Christ suffered on the cross, so you can suffer for an hour in church," I told her. But later, when I sat alone and pondered Christ's suffering, I wondered. *Do I really believe Jesus died on a cross to save my soul? Was he really God's Son? Who is God anyway?*

Everything I'd learned about God in the church scared me. Still, I began buying spiritual books to learn more about God.

Truthfully, I was ready to give up on him. The main reason? I wanted a divorce, and the Catholic Church teaches you shouldn't divorce.

God hates it if you leave your husband. So maybe it was time for me to leave God.

Health problems were also hounding me—fibromyalgia, panic attacks, and a breast cancer scare that ended with two surgeries and ultimately a benign diagnosis. My husband wasn't supportive through any of it. He took a mission out of town and was gone for weeks as I underwent the surgeries, with my wondering all the while if he even truly cared about me at all. My heart acted up, as well, so that was checked out. Too much caffeine, which made my heart gallop like a runaway horse. No surprise. I'd been living on coffee since I started writing for newspapers in my mid-twenties.

When Scott finally came home, he asked why I was so unhappy in our marriage. He was doing great, so what was wrong with me?

Away on missions, he would go out drinking with the other pilots, most of them divorced, remarried, or getting divorced again. Infidelity ran rampant in the military. I believed it was just a matter of time before my husband cheated on me. When I suggested getting breast implants after my surgeries—my breasts were small and battered, and I was so stressed out and bone-skinny—Scott was all for it. Even went with me to see a plastic surgeon for a consultation.

The doctor suggested the smallest cup size. "You're a thin, petite woman after all," he said.

"How about bigger cups?" Scott interjected with a grin.

Surprising myself, I insisted on the smaller implants. I didn't want to look like Dolly Parton. The doctor took a picture of my pre-surgery breasts, but not before picking up my cross necklace and placing it between my shoulder blades so it wouldn't show in the photo.

"We don't need this in the picture," he said with a tight smile.

With that, something in my spirit rebelled. I wanted to run out of the office right then, but there was another suspicious lump in my breast, and the doctor insisted on another biopsy before moving forward with the implants.

After another surgery with yet another benign diagnosis, I had new breasts that made my husband happy. That should have been good for our marriage, but it wasn't. I resented Scott more than ever.

And I was starting to die inside.

When I looked in the mirror, I didn't even recognize myself anymore. At the Sacramento Airport while waiting for a flight, a pilot approached me.

"Are you a movie star?" he asked, obviously smitten.

"No," I told him. "I write for a newspaper."

"You look like Pamela Anderson."

His flirting before we boarded the plane in Sacramento made me doubt his flying abilities. I was afraid he would be chasing a flight attendant around the cockpit instead of guiding the plane into San Diego. Sitting in coach, I pondered his mistaking me for a *Baywatch* babe. I didn't feel pretty. I felt plastic and fake, like my marriage.

The real battle arrived when Scott moved his mother in with us without even asking me, then turned around and left on a long military mission. I went out, covered newspaper stories, then returned home to write them while my mother-in-law cooked

Mexican food day and night, grease and flour flying all the way to the kitchen ceiling. She never cleaned up her magnificent messes. Just left it to me for when I got home from work after picking up the kids at day care.

Sometimes I came home to strange men sitting at our kitchen table. Big Momma cooked like nobody's business, but what she was really cooking up was hanky-panky. She adored younger men and was always trying to rouse up an affair. I just didn't get it. Who wants to sleep with strange men? The mailman, a guy she met on the bus, a lonely neighbor. They all had to be at least ten years younger than she was. Twenty years was better. My mother-in-law and men closer to my age than hers, laughing and flirting and feasting in my kitchen. I couldn't take any more.

My own marriage problems came to a head when Scott returned home from his mission. I can't even remember what started the explosion, but soon I was screaming, "F— your mother and F— you too!" in our front yard for all the world to hear.

Then I jumped in our SUV and gripped the steering wheel, shaking all over. I was so out of control, I hardly recognized myself.

"Mommy, you said the F-word really loud," my sweet little daughter, Cami, whispered from the backseat. I pressed my forehead to the steering wheel and closed my eyes. Everyone in our neighborhood had heard me hurling F-bombs. It was one of the lowest moments of my life.

Later, when I packed my bags to leave with my children, Scott stood in my way.

"You walk out that door, you go by yourself. You're not taking our kids out of my house."

I was a furious little wife half the size of my husband, staring at those big football muscles I'd loved while dating—now used to intimidate me. Let's face it, I was badly outgunned.

I carried my bags back to my closet, then walked into the girls' room, where Cami and Lacy sat on their beds, quietly playing with their dolls. Truth be told, Scott wasn't a bad father. He was gone a lot, but when he was home, he loved the kids.

The girls looked at me with wide innocent eyes as little Lacy asked, "Mommy, are you and Daddy okay?"

That question locked me inside my marriage. I didn't want to hurt my kids.

"We're okay, sweetie."

I kissed my girls, then walked into their baby brother's room and looked down at Luke sleeping in his crib. If we divorced, it would turn my children's lives upside down. Not just for the next few years but maybe for the rest of their lives. I couldn't imagine another woman mothering my children. Friends all around were divorcing—like a virus everyone was coming down with in our circle of friends.

One of my friends in San Diego had split with her husband. She walked out the door, and he wouldn't let her back in. One afternoon while he was at work, this friend and I climbed through a window into their house surrounded by palm trees. Pictures of her three small blond daughters smiling so innocently hung on the walls. I stood there for a minute looking at those little girls like this was a dream. A really bad dream. How could she stand being separated from her children even part time? We carried my friend's belongings to our cars. I had the family cat in my arms, lugging Kitty like a hostage to my white Toyota 4Runner—the whitest, fluffiest cat I'd ever seen.

After sticking that frightened feline in my car, I began to cry. How does life get this messed up—helping my friend escape her marriage like a convict breaking out of jail? This was the second time I'd shoved a frightened cat into my car, feeling as if my life was coming apart. I wanted to escape my own marriage too.

The next Saturday morning, after another raging fight with Scott, I loaded up the Toyota 4Runner—clothes, the kids' toys, and my computer. When I put the kids in the car, my husband climbed in too.

"What are you doing?" I asked.

"Going with you."

"Get out of the car," I whispered, not wanting the kids to hear me.

"We're a family," Scott said loudly from the passenger's seat. "We all go together."

He had figured out I was set on a ten-hour drive, exactly how long it took to get to the farm. If he wanted to ride along as a goodbye, then fly back to San Diego on Monday morning for his work, so be it. Three hours later, Cami had to pee.

"Grab the pee pot," Scott called back to her.

We didn't own a pee pot. But a minute later, our seven-year-old daughter was perched on top of a silver champagne bucket tinkling away, my view through the rearview mirror while driving. A month earlier, I had picked up the tarnished bucket at the San Diego Goodwill, purchased polish at the grocery store, and scrubbed my fingers to the bone making the silver bucket shine.

For our ten-year anniversary, I prepared a special shrimp scampi and steak dinner, and chilled a bottle of champagne in that bucket. We made it through a tense meal, barely touched the champagne, and a day later headed to Las Vegas, where I decided I needed that divorce. Now, I couldn't believe my eyes. Scott had turned our silver bucket into a pee pot for the girls.

"Oh, my gosh!" I cried. "That's our champagne bucket!"

"Not anymore," Scott said. "It's now our pee pot."

"This is so like our marriage! From champagne to pee!"

I hit the steering wheel with my fist, ready to burst into tears, but, to my surprise, both of us started laughing. I was so pissed (no pun intended) but laughing my head off.

Then we drove seven more hours without speaking to each other.

"Love is patient, love is kind. It does not envy, it does not boast, it is not proud ... love never fails" *(*1 Corinthians 13:4–8). At my parents' house, I read this Bible verse on the wall of my girlhood bedroom, where I crawled into bed that night weary to the bone. I was back safe and sound on the farm.

I tried not to look at those words on the wall. It had been an exhausting day. I just wanted to escape into sleep for the rest of my life. If I awoke, I wanted a divorce.

Chapter Fourteen

> I hope you live a life you're proud
> of. If you find that you are not,
> I hope you have the strength
> to start all over again.
>
> — F. Scott Fitzgerald

After trying to leave Scott without success, I took another job writing for a daily newspaper. We purchased a home in Northern California, ten hours away from Scott's work on Coronado Island. Monday mornings at five a.m., I would drive my husband to the Sacramento Airport. Plenty of weekends he didn't come home as he was off flying missions.

All around me, friends were divorcing. Their hot, new romances made me long for something new and exciting in my own life. My world consisted of writing and taking care of three little kids and more writing.

It was a lonely time for me.

Contemplating divorce again, I finally felt grown up. Coffee and wine had become habits, and books filled every nook and cranny of my house. Each time we moved, Scott threatened to dump all my books in the trash, but he always ended up carrying boxes of them wherever I wanted. Maybe that was why I hadn't left him yet—he was strong, and he let me read.

He also said, "You walk out that door, you leave by yourself. I'm keeping the kids, but you can take all your stupid books with you."

I couldn't leave without the kids, so I stayed put for the time being, finding romance in novels when I wasn't writing. Mostly, though, I was writing. Books that didn't sell and newspaper articles perhaps a few hundred people read. I did get to do some really cool stories on the U-2 spy plane out at Beale Air Force Base. I rode in chase cars with the pilots and went on their survival training missions in the mountains. But, on the whole, I covered mom-and-pop stories for the newspaper. *"The Patterson family carved five-hundred pumpkins and lined the road with jack-o-lanterns. Drive by on Halloween night to see all the glimmering gourds."*

Here and there in desperation, I said little prayers to God, which usually brought more than I bargained for. With my husband away at a three-month military school, I found myself drinking more than usual—staying up late writing and sucking down wine after putting the kids to bed. Dragging myself out of the sack in the morning to get the girls to school had become so difficult.

One afternoon I stopped at the store to buy another bottle of sauvignon blanc. I wanted to drink and write that night and had no wine left in my fridge. After buying the blanc and TV dinners for the kids, I drove home feeling bereft.

How had my life ended up this way?

I wasn't a great writer but did have a New York literary agent trying to sell my novels. My agent was even talking to producers in Hollywood about turning one of my books into a movie. Julia Roberts's film company had the manuscript. Supposedly Roberts herself was reading the novel. I had a hard time believing that. The newspaper I worked for really liked me. My editor told me all the time how special I was, but I didn't feel special. I felt like a failure.

Finding childcare for Luke and still nursing morning, noon, and night so I could cover newspaper stories between nursing left me strung-out. Luke cried when I dropped him off with a babysitter. My mom helped with the kids, but she worked all day at the hospital. This made it difficult for me to pursue a career of my own. I'd already tried day care with the girls. It was torture for all of us. More and more, I felt like I needed to give up writing and just focus on being a mom. And my habit of wine drinking while writing at night after putting the kids to bed had really begun to bother me. Was I becoming an alcoholic? I didn't think drinking made me a better writer. Actually, it made me weep while writing, bringing out emotions I usually stuffed down deep during the day when I was sober.

As I got out of my car in the garage with that bottle of wine in one hand and a bag of TV dinners in the other, I whispered a prayer of desperation.

God, help me stop drinking alone at night.

As soon as the prayer left my lips, that bottle fell right out of my grasp and exploded on the concrete at my feet. Wine and glass shards splattered my sandals and jeans. I was shocked. It felt as if someone really strong yanked that bottle from my hand.

As I carried the TV dinners into the house, then returned to clean up the mess in the garage, my knees trembled. Something happened in the garage—a force I had no control over ripped that bottle away, making me suddenly and painfully aware of a higher power. I felt small and somewhat psychotic as I cleaned up the glass and wine.

God, if that was you, get me through this night without wine.

I couldn't remember the last time I hadn't drunk before falling into bed exhausted after writing—often till midnight or later. With no wine, I didn't write that night. After tucking the kids into bed, I knelt beside my own bed and earnestly prayed for the first time in a long time.

After that night, I began to pray more often. Not the memorized prayers of my Catholic girlhood but heartfelt prayers for God to help me. Instead of scrambling for a babysitter to cover for me as I wrote my stories, I told my newspaper editor I couldn't write the features anymore. I took my toddler son to the park instead, enjoying the sunshine with Luke. Without drinking at night and going to bed earlier, I listened to the birds sing in the morning. Feeling more alive and awake than I had in years, I noticed butterflies and ladybugs and people walking their dogs at the park.

The world had a lot of happy dogs.

Now that I wasn't writing and drinking, I began to long for grown-up company at night. I was sober but lonely. Friends perceived my longing for companionship and invited me out on the town. Scott was always away on flying missions. One night after dropping the kids off at the farm, I dressed up and headed for a dinner club where singles mingled and the married slipped toward divorce. The music was loud, the dance floor hopping. I felt ridiculously out of place the moment I stepped through the door.

Before I even sat down at a table, the waitress walked over and said, "This is for you from that gentleman sitting over there." She handed me a glass of white wine.

I avoided looking at the man and sipped the white wine slowly because I wanted to drive home. I turned down invitations to dance until one of my girlfriends told me to just go home.

"You're no fun. If you're not going to dance with anyone, you should just leave."

I knew she was right. I didn't want to spoil anyone's good time. The next guy that walked over to our table, I took his hand and let him lead me onto the dance floor. His smile was bright on his swarthy face. His English was thick with a Spanish accent. He said he was in America on business, coming here to encourage California rice farmers to consider growing olives instead. I wasn't sure I heard him correctly. Was he talking about growing olives in Spain or California?

The pounding music suddenly slowed. I tried not to stiffen when the Spaniard wrapped a bold arm around my waist and drew me close. It felt so strange to let another man hold me. I hadn't been in anyone else's arms since I was nineteen years old.

In that Spaniard's embrace, a memory came to mind of Scott's confession when I was pregnant with our son. How he went out with his pilot friends while on a mission and spent the night dancing with a woman named Jeannine. The same name as his sister. I was still so wounded over that.

"I didn't go home with her," Scott assured me, as if that was the important thing. "We just danced all night," he explained as I sobbed in a parking lot, holding my pregnant belly and crying unabashedly before he left on another mission.

More than two years had passed since my husband's confession in that parking lot, but I hadn't forgotten it. I was about to get even with a sexy Spaniard.

Chapter Fifteen

And as to me, I know nothing else but miracles.
— Walt Whitman, *Leaves of Grass*

I used to think the voice of God would sound very old, very wise, and very strict. But when it came to me on that dance floor in the arms of the Spaniard, it sounded matter-of-fact and a voice I didn't recognize as my own. The song "Do You Believe in Life after Love?" by Cher had just played, and the DJ was slowing things down again. The Spaniard tucked me up against his chest as I was thinking. *I do believe in life after love. I believe I will be happy after I divorce my husband.*

Be brave, I told myself. *Let your hair down. Let yourself go. Just be happy.*

Then the voice of God whispered. *Look around. Nobody is happy here. It's all a lie.*

I had thoughts all the time, but this thought was distinctly different. I knew without a doubt that it was God. For a moment the veil was lifted, and I saw desperate souls instead of happy dancers. The vision stunned me.

"I'm sorry, I have to go." I pushed away the Spaniard.

He called my name in pleading Spanish, but I walked away as fast as I could and didn't look back.

I grabbed my purse off the chair and longed to break into a sprint for the door, but I forced myself to act normal.

Breathe. Walk. Just breathe and walk.

It was a good idea since I was wearing high heels. I'd never been graceful in heels. A woman who walks normally in heels is a rare thing.

When I finally slid behind the wheel of my white Toyota 4Runner, I felt some relief. I just wanted to get home—to go to bed and sleep off hearing the voice of God, the way you'd sleep off a hangover.

I must have imagined it. God didn't talk to people in bars. *Maybe I'd had too much to drink. Should I even be driving? Hell, yes, I was driving! I had to get out of there. I had to speed away from the voice of God.*

Alone in my king-size bed, I stared at the ceiling, my eyes wide with fear. The kids were at the farm with my folks. And who knew where my husband was tonight, probably dancing at some bar with a woman named Jeannine. I had always thought of myself as a forgiving person, but, slowly, the years had revealed I wasn't. I hadn't forgiven Scott for dancing with Jeannine when I was pregnant with our son, but I'd finally gotten even. I'd danced with a Spaniard. But getting even left me feeling awful. I regretted dancing with another man. I was married. That was foolish. And was that really God speaking to me?

God, if you're real, I need you.

That simple, heartfelt prayer brought a flood of tears.

I wasn't at the end of myself yet, but I was getting there. I sobbed myself to sleep and woke the next morning to a roomful of sunshine. I'd made it through the night. Thank God for the morning.

After collecting my kids from the farm, I spent the rest of the weekend just being their mom. My idea of a "mom" didn't dance with Spaniards. She didn't go to bars at all. So, in the weeks that followed, I gave up on bars and went to church instead. In the wake of saying, "God, if you're real, I need you," freaky things started happening.

Scott came home for a weekend, and we tried going on a date. At my insistence we visited a Christian bookstore and bought two books: *Winning Your Husband Back Before It's Too Late* and *Winning Your Wife Back Before It's Too Late* by Gary Smalley. Then, we barely survived dinner. I really didn't want to read the *Winning Your Husband Back* book, but I did want Scott to read the wife book. Of course, he didn't read it, and, reluctantly, I found myself reading the husband book.

By the end of it, I was crying. Not about my husband but about God. I wanted a relationship with the God this book talked about. I'd never read Protestant books. Just as I didn't go to Protestant churches except for weddings. I found it kind of ironic that a Protestant book about marriage would change my views about divorce.

I enrolled my girls in a Catholic school and began attending daily Mass. I took my toddler along, Luke dressed like a cowboy in boots, hat, and leather chaps strapped to his skinny, little legs. At home he watched endless bull-riding videos—real clips of real bull rides. Don't ask me what I was thinking. Obviously, I wasn't thinking like a mother, so Luke believed he was a bull rider. He was blond, about three feet tall, and cute as they come. Everywhere he went he carried a leather strap to tie himself to just about everything, the way a real bull rider would. In church he tied himself to the knee rest while I kneeled and prayed. As the priest conducted Mass, Luke pushed his hat down tight, raised one arm in the air, and wrapped five little fingers around the strap he'd secured to the knee rest.

"Let 'er go, boys," he whispered loudly because he knew he was supposed to be quiet in church.

Then he bounced up and down on the knee rest, making an awful clatter as he imagined himself staying on the bull for eight seconds.

I was just trying to have faith for those eight seconds, hoping God would speak to me again like he did that night in the bar. Well, not like that night in the bar. I wanted more than a strange thought piercing my soul like the sword of God. I wanted to know God. The God of the Protestant books I was reading.

There were no young moms around me in the pews at daily Mass. In fact, I was the only mom with a little one there. Old people surrounded us, some smiling in delight at my toddler son in his cowboy gear riding the knee rest and others scowling at us. I ignored everyone—I was trying to connect with God. When the connection didn't happen, I left church, discouraged.

The next day was October 4, the Feast Day of St. Francis and the "Blessing of the Animals." The girls' school participated with the church, and there we were, standing on the lawn between the school and the cathedral getting our little black-and-white dog blessed by the priest. After that, I carried Fifi back to the car. She was shaking up a storm like nervous little dogs do when sprinkled with holy water. Luke scampered off to play with other small children on the playground.

The girls had followed their teachers to class, and a group of moms stood near the little ones. I was the new mom on campus. I wanted to just slip by the other moms and grab my itty-bitty cowboy and get the heck out of there, but I couldn't be rude. I stopped among the circle of women.

"So, you're Cami's mom," a bubbly blonde said to me. "My son is in Cami's class. We just got a cocker spaniel puppy, and my son named her Cami. Isn't that the cutest thing?"

All the moms were smiling, agreeing that it was the cutest thing ever. I knew this mom's name was Fifi, and I had just stuck our Fifi in the car. Before I could stop myself, the words spewed out. "That's funny. Cami's little dog is Fifi."

The bubbly blonde's smile froze on her face. An awkward silence gripped the group. I felt as if I had just stepped in gum or something worse.

"Oh, don't say it," Fifi's voice sharpened. "Your dog is a poodle, isn't it? I hate poodles!"

I didn't know Fifi, but I could tell she was really annoyed.

"No, she's a rat terrier," I said, relieved we didn't own a poodle.

Another mom put her hand over her mouth to smother her laughter. The other moms lost their smiles as Fifi's mouth hung open as if I'd just slapped her. Feeling beyond awkward, I gave up and went to fetch Luke. He had tied himself on to a piece of playground equipment, doing his eight-second routine.

Back at the car, I buckled Luke into his car seat as Fifi curled up next to him, her shaking abated. As we drove away from the school, I turned on the radio. Recently, I'd discovered Christian music, which I had never listened to before.

God, if you're real, please play that Chris Rice song, "Smell the Color 9" for me. I really need to know you're real.

To my shock, it was the next song on the radio.

When Scott came home, I tried to talk to him about God. He halfway listened, then said, "You're getting really religious. If this helps you, good."

I assumed he was really saying "If religion keeps you from divorcing me, I'm happy with that." And our talk about God went absolutely nowhere. It was as if he'd gotten up and left the table but still sat there staring at me. All the goodwill was gone from our conversation. I felt so disheartened.

Later in bed, we had sex—two bodies connecting with our hearts miles apart. Afterward, without any conversation, my husband rolled over and went to sleep. That had always bugged me. How easily Scott slept, lying there on his back in the same position all night long like a log in the forest. I tossed and turned through a hundred positions, twisting the covers into a knotted mess. I was as high-strung in sleep as I was in life. It didn't seem fair.

Why am I this way?

It's true, I came from a long line of high-strung people, but there had to be an escape from this stressful life.

I'd begun to search for escape in a search for God.

Unable to close my eyes, I picked up one of my Protestant books from the nightstand and read with a flashlight. What I'd discovered in these books was a God of love that didn't fit my

Catholic God of judgment. And this God of love was accessible to me not through a priest as I'd been taught but through a real one-on-one relationship.

It made sense.

In the past, my God encounters had come one-on-one after heartfelt prayers, not due to reciting the memorized verses of my Catholic youth. And God had come to me not when I was at my best but at my worst—at the lowest moments of my life, this God of love had revealed himself to me. I hadn't been able to earn God's love. It had always been free. It was like answering the door as your most pitiful self and finding God standing there.

Who wants to meet God when you look like hell? Feel like hell? Belong in hell?

A sinner without any grace of your own. A beggar who deserves death but is given life instead by this God of love.

This really frustrated me about God. I wanted to meet him in my best clothes when he came to the door. I wanted to welcome God with my own righteousness, which God called "filthy rags." It was all in the books I was reading. But God didn't come to me when I was at my best. He always came at my worst. When I hit rock bottom and lay there helpless in the mess I had made of my life. Maybe because that was when I really cried out to him with all my heart, pleading with him to help me. But it was more than that.

God was a beggar's God.

The God of ragamuffins as Brennan Manning said in his *Ragamuffin Gospel*. The first time I read Brennan Manning, I couldn't accept his view of God the loving Father God, Abba. It wasn't really Abba I had a problem with. It was Manning, the priest who gave up being a priest to marry the love of his life and who then lived so selfishly on all that free grace, he destroyed his marriage.

Manning's been accused of spreading cheap grace. I agree and disagree. Cheap was there on the part of Manning—a drunk with narcissistic tendencies for much of his life, according to Manning himself—but grace was there too, on the part of God, the ragamuffin's Abba God.

Learning about Abba was a whole new mind-set for me. This Father God who loved the prodigal son, the kid who took his inheritance and squandered it all on wine, women, and song, then found himself feeding someone else's pigs for a living. He ended up so hungry, all that kid wanted was to eat the pig's rotten food right out of the trough with the animals. So, he decided to go home, casting all his hope on his father's loving grace.

I got that story. I had raised pigs for 4-H.

The problem I kept running into being raised Catholic was that the prodigal son never got grace. He got ten Hail Marys and perhaps some Our Fathers too.

Do something to help yourself, sinner. But I knew I couldn't help myself.

"You can't turn a sow's ear into a silk purse," Grandma Helen used to say.

I knew I was a sow's ear, and I desperately needed saving.

But I couldn't save myself.

Chapter Sixteen

We are all broken. That's how the light gets in.
— Ernest Hemingway

When Scott and I fought on the weekends he came home from his missions, after the kids went to bed, I'd pack some clothes in a brown grocery sack and sleep at my brother's house. At dawn, I'd return home before my little ones woke up, pretending everything was fine. One Saturday evening, Scott took me on a shopping date. That was so rare. He hated shopping, and, even stranger, he marched me into a luggage store.

"What are we doing here?" I asked.

He picked up a little leather suitcase. Really nice but really expensive.

"Do you like this one?"

"Yes."

"Good," he said and carried it to the counter.

After buying it, he treated me to dinner. We didn't talk about the suitcase until we finished eating.

"I bought you that suitcase because I'm tired of watching you walk out the door with your panties in a grocery sack. The next time you leave, you'll have nice Flyaway gear."

Flyaway was the army duffel Scott used on his flight missions. All military pilots had Flyaway gear. A ready-packed bag to leave on a moment's notice.

After that shopping trip, I began to genuinely pray for my marriage. I still pretty much wanted a divorce, but the next time we got into a fight, I had my little suitcase with me. That suitcase reminded me that my husband had a sweet side.

One night, while praying alone in my bedroom, I heard God say, *Do not divorce your husband. Love him as I have loved you.*

I didn't hear the words audibly, but God's voice came to me as a thought I didn't recognize as my own. And it was very convicting. Of all the things for God to put his finger on. Divorce. The one thing I fantasized about all the time—the thing I desperately wanted.

When Scott came home, I was good to him. Even when he upset me, I didn't pick up my Flyaway gear and leave. I stayed in our bed. I knew my husband valued me, but I wasn't convinced he loved me. And when you're married to a soldier, life can get pretty lonely.

A few years earlier, before Luke was born, Scott spent several months in a Blackhawk helicopter looking for survivors in the floodwaters and taxiing officials around California so they could figure out where to dump the relief money. When the Sacramento

Valley flooded, friends and family rolled up my parents' hill to the farm. In total, fifty-five people with thirty-five dogs, three cats, and a handful of RV trailers escaped to the Sutter Buttes.

That wasn't including the people and dogs in the RV trailers parked around the house. Fifty-five people slept inside my parents' three-bedroom, two-story ranch house. Entire families holed up in bedrooms, piles of kids in closets, the living room floor covered with bodies. I slept with my little daughters in an attic, wall-to-wall with other relatives. My uncle snored like a machine gun. I lay awake in a sleeping bag listening to him as rain pounded the roof ... suspecting I was pregnant.

The next day, running out of food, my cousin and I walked from room to room with a list, writing down everything people wanted us to buy. Beer, beer, wine, beer, whiskey, beer, wine, beer, and more whiskey.

"What about food?" I asked.

Some of them weren't even drinkers. Like my great-aunt who never took a drink but said, "Buy lots of rice. And don't forget the wine, honey."

With a wad of cash collected from everyone, my cousin and I drove north, away from the evacuated towns, until we found an open grocery store. My cousin, in her mid-twenties, was pretty and blond with a great personality. Two carts full of alcohol and a few bags of rice later, we stood at the checkout line waiting to be rung up. I had slipped a pregnancy test into one of the carts among the beer.

Like everyone else stuck on the hill—sleeping on top of one another and anxious over the possible flood—I was ready to get drunk and forget about my problems, at least for the night.

But in church, at Christmastime a few weeks earlier, I had prayed for a son. We had our darling girls, but I desperately wanted a little boy. Scott wasn't interested in having more children. The only thing he cared about was flying. Walking out of Mass that Sunday before Christmas, a lady selling raffle tickets stopped me.

"Have you gotten your tickets yet for our annual holiday fundraiser?" she asked sweetly. "Look at our prize this year. Isn't it beautiful?"

On a table by the door in the church lobby sat a large baby-blue wicker basket filled with gourmet food. When I saw the basket, I thought it would be perfect to hold a baby boy. Both my girls had slept in a basket when they were infants—an old wicker thing I found at an antique store in Alabama while Scott was stationed at Fort Rucker learning to fly. I scrubbed the basket clean, then spray-painted it white, sewing a padded insert myself and covering the inside with soft cotton.

"So, are you going to buy a ticket? It's a dollar a ticket, but I recommend buying at least ten for a chance to win this fabulous basket," the lady prompted me.

She suddenly didn't sound as sweet. I only had four quarters left in my purse. I had a twenty-dollar bill, but when the donation basket rolled around, I felt a definite nudge to put the twenty in the basket. I didn't want to part with my twenty dollars. I'd planned on putting the four quarters in the basket instead. Like a lot of people in church, a dollar usually seemed good enough.

"I only have four quarters," I said to the lady.

She frowned at me.

I dug the four quarters out of my purse, and the lady grudgingly handed me one ticket.

A week later, I got a phone call. "Congratulations! You won the church basket!"

"Wow! I only bought one ticket," I told the lady on the phone.

Silence. And then a restrained, "You're the lady with four quarters, aren't you?"

It was the ticket lady on the phone. I knew she didn't like me. I swallowed hard. "Yes, it's me," I sheepishly admitted.

"Meet me at the church in an hour to pick up your basket." Then she abruptly hung up.

The last thing I wanted to do was go get the basket from that lady. I'd spent my whole life trying to be liked. Groveling to be liked. Working my fanny off to be liked by other women. I wasn't sure why. Perhaps because in kindergarten I was bullied by some older girls who would lock me in the bathroom and make me talk—I had a speech impediment and couldn't say my S's.

When they demanded I say "babysit," I would say "baby tit," and they'd laugh their butts off. I did my best to make those bully girls like me. They finally left me alone after I won their affection. They became great protectors, and eventually nobody teased me at school anymore about my speech problem.

When I got to the church parking lot, the lady already had her trunk open. The basket was waiting for me like a promise from God. When we loaded it into the back of my Toyota 4Runner, all I could think was, *God is going to put a baby boy in this beautiful baby-blue basket for me this year.*

I was nice to the ticket lady. I kind of felt sorry for her. I could tell she didn't want me to have the basket. I almost explained what winning the basket meant to me—that God was going to give me a baby boy—but her mouth was firmly set and her eyes shone with dislike. I decided it wasn't worth bothering to try to win her over.

A month later, I was standing in line at the grocery store behind my cousin who was paying for all that booze and a few bags of rice. She was talking with the cute checkout guy, and they were hitting it off. So, I picked up a *People* magazine and began browsing the stories. I loved *People*. Especially the pieces they sometimes printed about famous authors. I dreamed of becoming a novelist one day.

I already knew God had put a baby boy in my womb. I knew it the moment I won that basket at church.

"Do you want to use this coupon now?" I heard the checkout guy ask my cousin. She was chatting with him, a big smile on her face.

In his hand, he held the pregnancy test.

"What?" My cousin was suddenly very confused.

"This pregnancy test has a coupon on it. Do you want to use the coupon?"

Funny how quickly he stopped flirting with her. He held up the pregnancy test, staring at my cousin like she was some kind of wild thing.

"Paula!" My cousin blurted. "Get over here, now!"

I couldn't stop laughing. "Do you want to use the coupon?" I asked my cousin.

"Are you pregnant?" the clerk asked.

My cousin then turned from me and faced the cute checkout guy. "That is not mine! It's hers!"

When we got back to the house, we handed out all the alcohol to the flood refugees. They popped beer cans and wine corks like it was New Year's Eve—which had occurred about a week earlier. Upstairs, away from the desperate crowd, my cousin stood at the bathroom door while I took the test. I really didn't want to tell her the results when I walked out. She was just a year younger than me and longed to meet the man of her dreams and have babies. I already had two kids and had been a wife for eight years.

"It's positive," I whispered.

Tears flooded my cousin's eyes. "I'm so happy for you." We hugged. "I hope your hubby calls you tonight so you can tell him the good news," my cousin said as she wiped her eyes.

"I hope so too." I wanted to cry as well.

But Scott didn't call that night as I watched everyone drinking up a storm. I was thrilled to be pregnant but feared he wouldn't be happy. A day later, the levee in town broke and floodwaters swept the valley. Days after this, Scott finally called.

"I'm pregnant," I told him through tears—partly because of the baby and partly because it had been more than a week since he had last called me.

"I saw a cow on a roof today," he responded.

"Did you hear what I said?"

"Yes, you're pregnant. But I saw a cow on a roof today. I haven't saved anyone yet, but we've found people in trees and on rooftops, and animals are on the roofs. This flood is amazing."

What amazed *me* was that my husband didn't seem to care that we were having a baby.

Luke was born on a hot September day. Scott had been flying nonstop drug missions, searching for illegal marijuana farms up and down the state. Because his child was being born, he was with me at the hospital instead of in the helicopter he routinely flew. Another pilot was in the cockpit when that helicopter stopped working high in the sky. The pilot was a Vietnam vet who had been flying helicopters since before Scott was born. That older and more experienced pilot auto-rotated and survived the crash. Scott got the call at the hospital that his helicopter had fallen from the sky.

"If Luke hadn't been born, I'd be dead," he told me as we stared at our newborn son in wonder. "I couldn't have landed in those woods like Henry did. That kind of malfunction is beyond my skills. Good thing it happened to a Vietnam vet."

Scott was suddenly displaying a humility I hadn't seen in him in a long time. He embraced the baby that kept him alive, declaring he wanted to fly less and father his children more. Still, in just a few short months, he left for flight school to learn how to fly Blackhawk helicopters. His dream come true. More aviation schools followed, along with the Army's Advanced Course.

He was gone a long time.

Chapter Seventeen

Faith doesn't make sense, it makes miracles.
— Tony Evans

We celebrated Luke's first birthday without his dad there. Scott was in another state taking more classes on Blackhawks. Another year went by with Luke a busy toddler and me a devout Catholic now going to church every day. With my husband away more than ever, I prayed, "Please, Lord, change our life. Do something amazing."

As God answered my little prayers, my faith was growing strong enough to pray bigger prayers.

The next time Scott came home from a flying mission, he said, "I looked into ROTC jobs in California. There was a spot at UC Davis, but they just filled it."

"You'd give up flying to teach ROTC?" I couldn't believe I was hearing him correctly.

"ROTC would be a good change for our family." Scott's blue eyes softened. "I've been thinking about taking a break from flying for us. An ROTC teaching job would put me home every night."

"I don't want to move," I told him. In the Army a change in career always came with a move.

"I'm looking at a position at a school up in Washington State," he admitted.

"I'm not going to Washington." I braced myself for a fight.

Scott left the room without another word. After he was gone, I felt bad about shooting him down so quickly.

That night I prayed, "Please, God, give Scott that UC Davis job."

Davis was only an hour and a half from my parents' farm.

A week later, Scott came home with a big smile on his face. "You're not going to believe this. The Davis job opened up again. The guy they hired didn't work out. I have an interview on Monday."

I nearly passed out. I could hardly believe it. God was answering my big prayers.

I'd read at least ten books on how to know God, and I was now attending daily Mass, Luke in his cowboy gear riding the knee rest at my feet every morning. The same week my husband got the interview in Davis, a young Passionist priest, Father Cedric Pisegna, passed through our town teaching about the Holy Spirit. Because I was spending so much time at Mass, I would hear every word Father Cedric preached.

Farming Grace

At night I attended Father Cedric's missions by myself. It was easier to listen without Luke doing his eight seconds.

I begged and pleaded with Scott to go on the weekend with me—I'd never heard anything like what Father Cedric was saying in church. My husband dragged his feet but went and sat beside me for the Saturday night service.

"If this priest was here every Sunday, I would go with you. He's really good," Scott said after the Mass. But minutes later, he was over it.

Personally, I couldn't believe the story Father Cedric told of how he was "saved." I had never heard a Catholic priest talk about salvation before. This was evangelical talk. I knew because I was still reading about being born again in the Protestant books piling up on my nightstand. Father Cedric said Catholics needed to be born again too. He read this straight out of the Bible to us in church.

"You should not be surprised at my saying 'You must be born again'" (John 3:7). Then he told of the night the Holy Spirit came to his bedroom, and he was born again in a swirl of dazzling light.

After hearing this, I longed to be born again in a swirl of dazzling light too. I remembered the white light shooting out of the statue when I saw the vision a few years back in church. I prayed night and day, pleading with God to send his Holy Spirit to me. Maybe it would come in a piercing white light. Did people really see the light this way?

In December Scott came home and handed me a beautiful marriage Bible.

"Happy birthday, babe," he said.

The gift blew me away. Almost as much as my husband then announcing he had gotten the ROTC job in Davis.

"Where did you find this Bible?" I couldn't imagine Scott walking into a Christian bookstore by himself. He'd never liked Christians.

"At a Christian bookstore," he grinned, and his dimples split his cheeks. I loved it when he smiled wide-open that way.

"And you got the job? Really? That's amazing." I hugged him. Then he kissed me all-out, the way he'd kissed me when we were young—and in love.

Two weeks later I was still so happy about Scott giving up flying and buying me a Bible. That night, our rat terrier puppy, Sophie—Fifi's daughter—woke me up at three a.m. I heard her whining in her kennel, so I walked downstairs and took her outside to the bathroom. Staring up into the starry night—a bright and cold December morning with my breath swirling white around my face—the greatness of God suddenly and completely overwhelmed me. It was as if the sky electrified and the distance between heaven and earth dissolved in an instant.

God was there.

Fear like I'd never known washed over me.

I quickly gathered up Sophie, ran inside, and stuffed her back into her kennel. Then I dashed upstairs and jumped into bed, shaking like a leaf. I knew God was real. Suddenly and completely knew it deep in my bones. Deep in my soul. And I was scared to death.

I had just turned thirty-three years old and had never really read the Bible, though for the past two weeks I had been browsing my birthday gift. There was nothing good in me, I knew in that moment. Oh, how I knew I was a sinner. Only God was good. Human beings were not good.

Father Cedric said if you wake in the middle of the night, invite the Holy Spirit to come to you. With blankets tucked tightly under my chin, I asked God to send his Holy Spirit to me.

And then I saw the light.

A bright, swirling white light slowly entered our bedroom.

Ask for forgiveness. The command came not in an audible voice, but it was so real coming from the light, my heart pounded out of my chest. I thought I might be dying.

"Please, forgive me," I whispered, looking away from that beautiful light.

I knew my earthly eyes couldn't handle that heavenly light. I decided I must be on the verge of death to see such a brilliant sight.

You're forgiven, beloved, I heard as the light came closer, swirling in our bedroom.

I don't know how long it stayed there. I closed my eyes, but even with my eyes shut, I could see that amazing light and hear the sound of a roaring wind. Except there was no wind. The room was still, as when I was outside and suddenly knew God was real when I looked up at the stars. The stillness was so startling. So powerful. So timeless. It had no beginning and no end.

I was being born again on this starry night just days before Christmas. My husband slept through the whole thing. After the light gently left the room, I woke him up to tell him God had just visited us.

Scott looked at me as if I'd lost my mind

"Something supernatural has happened," Scott admitted the day after I saw the light in our bedroom. "I don't know what it was, but I see your soul in your eyes now."

It was such a strange thing for him to say as we lay in bed talking more than we had in years. I was doing my best to convince him Jesus was alive. That God had paid us a visit. I was going to heaven now and wanted Scott to go too.

"I don't know what I believe about God." Scott said, and then made love to me after telling me I had a beautiful soul. It wasn't the soulless sex we'd fallen into in our marriage. I felt a shift in the atmosphere, deep calling to deep, but Scott didn't get it yet.

What my husband couldn't explain in the months that followed was how much I changed. One of the first things I did was quit my newspaper job and call my literary agent in New York City to tell him I couldn't write anymore. Everything I used to know fell away. My pride crumbled. I cried a lot. I gave up on my career and picked four-leaf clovers from our yard with my children, no longer believing in luck.

All I wanted was Jesus.

"I'm going to grow a garden instead of writing," I softly told Scott after several days of prayers and tears and clover picking. I knew Jesus wanted me to concentrate on being a good wife and mom, and I couldn't write and also do those things well. Maybe the garden was my idea. I didn't know what to do with my energy after I gave up my greatest love—writing—for the Lord's greater love.

A resurrection of the love I once felt for my husband was needed now. It seemed impossible, but I knew it was imperative. When Scott gave up flying and took the ROTC job, he did it to save our marriage, which was a big sacrifice on his part. Now, it was my turn. I tucked my computer into the closet as tears drenched my face. It was like burying my best friend. I couldn't help it. Writing was my thing.

A mourning period followed.

At daily Mass I stared at the large crucifix behind the altar. Luke bounced around in his cowboy gear as tears coursed down my cheeks. My dreams of becoming an author were dying, but maybe my marriage would live. "Unless a kernel of wheat falls to the ground and dies, it remains only a single seed. But if it dies, it produces many seeds" (John 12:24).

The verse stayed with me as I prepared a place in our backyard for a garden while praying that God would renew my love for my husband.

I know the movies tell us true love doesn't try. It just *is*. True love is perfect all by itself without even trying. Isn't that something? Doesn't it sound so good? It's also completely untrue. The truth is, real love takes real work. Real sacrifice. There may be seasons in your marriage when you just die to yourself every day to keep your marriage alive. Days where you get out of bed and look at your spouse standing in front of the coffeemaker in his boxer shorts scratching his privates and you think *I can't do this another day. I can't last one more day in this kitchen.*

I've been there, and I can tell you that you *can* last another day in your kitchen. In your marriage. You can do all things through Christ who gives you strength (Philippians 4:16). Say you're sorry. Say your prayers. Say: If God is for us who can be against us? (Romans 8:31). Pull out your Bible and read it. Believe it. Live it. Let faith in Jesus change you. Let faith in Jesus change your marriage.

Chapter Eighteen

What lies behind us and what lies before us are tiny matters compared to what lies within us.
— Ralph Waldo Emerson

Instead of throwing in the towel and getting that divorce, we pulled up in front of a funky little house with a couch on the porch where Scott announced, "This is our new home."

My heart sank, but I didn't voice my disappointment. We'd just sold our lovely two-story house an hour away, and Scott was starting his ROTC job teaching military history at UC Davis. The house was a rental a few miles from the college. Four college boys were moving out so we could move in.

"It's so nice of them to leave that couch for us there." I was thinking how our three small children would look jumping up and down on that broken-down thing for all the neighbors to see.

With Scott in the Army, we had lived a lot of different places in the past twelve years, but never had there been living room furniture on the front porch of any of our homes.

"The couch will be gone by the time our stuff gets here." Scott pointed to a nearby park. "We can walk the kids down there every night to play. I'll be home for dinner now. Won't that be great?"

My throat tightened. I found it hard to swallow. I wasn't sure I wanted my husband home every night. For years he'd been away on missions. I knew God wanted me to stop thinking about divorce and also to stop writing to just be a mom, a wife, and a follower of Jesus. But every bit of my self-worth was tied up in my writing. Giving it up terrified me. And my husband being home every night scared me even more.

Honestly, I wasn't sure I liked Scott anymore.

He'd become a true Army officer, always bossing me around. I felt like I didn't really know him. But I heard the daily whisper of Jesus inviting me to give up focusing on my own happiness and to focus on loving God and loving my husband.

Once we moved into that rental house, I didn't care much anymore about where we lived, though I cleaned it like a madwoman. We shared the space with bugs, mice, and perhaps a raccoon once we settled into that rattrap place. Literally, I set traps everywhere.

Scott put a foosball table in the middle of the living room. Each night, he and the kids would play, Luke standing on a milk crate, loudly slamming that little ball around, laughing and loving being together while I plugged my ears and tried to pray.

Please, God, restore our marriage and help me like this dirty old house and that stupid foosball table in our living room.

When my mother-in-law came to visit, she was horrified by where we lived. "How could you sell your beautiful home for this little dump?" She looked around at the battered rental, the jungle in the backyard, and threw up her hands. "You must really love my son to live here for him."

I kept my mouth shut, not feelin' the love. I felt tested. This was something new I was learning. To give thanks for a roof over my head and three little kids safe in their beds. Children so happy to have their dad home every night to play with them before bedtime.

"This house isn't so bad," Scott said a few weeks into our new life in Davis. "If we clean up the backyard, we can sit out there around a fire pit. The kids can make s'mores, and we can talk and share a glass of wine." Scott's blue eyes sparkled with longing as he looked at me.

"We should have kept that couch and put it out there too. The kids and critters would like that in this junkyard," I said, smiling back at him. I sensed God's work in my husband and in me.

Scott laughed, and it hit me how handsome he was in that moment. After several weeks of no writing, going to daily Mass, hanging out with three-year-old Luke at the park, and walking to the school to get the girls, my heart had softened toward my husband and our new home.

"How about we put the foosball table out in the backyard? You guys make a ton of noise playing that game at night in the house."

"I like it in the living room," Scott said. "It's a lot better than zoning out in front of the TV. Besides, we can't play out in the yard in the dark."

"Tarzan might join you out there," I said, looking at all the lush green vines covering the backyard trees and the forest of weeds that was once a lawn.

"We'll work on the yard this weekend," Scott promised.

Within a month, we were sitting in the yard, circled around a fire pit as a family. We nearly had a lawn by now, and I was working on that spot for my garden. I didn't know a thing about gardening, but when I unearthed our first little carrot that summer, it felt like a new beginning. I also loved watching Scott become the dad I never thought he could be. The husband I never thought he could be. God was answering all those prayers I'd been lifting up. I was falling in love with Scott all over again.

Then 9/11 happened, and I thought I would lose my husband to a war.

Yet, the Army allowed him to stay at the university teaching cadets instead of sticking him back into the cockpit of a Blackhawk. I cried when Scott's cadets graduated and were sent into battle in Afghanistan. I also cried when Scott arrived home safely every night. I cried because I loved walking to the park with our family each evening, and I loved sitting around our fire pit in the backyard at night. I told myself I loved listening to my husband and our children laughing in the living room as they beat the foosball table to death—I was still trying to fall in love with that.

I never succeeded in trapping all the critters scurrying through that rental house night and day. Once, a mouse ran over the top of my slipper as I ate breakfast at the kitchen table, but that albatross of a house became our home. The place where our family started over and the war in Afghanistan passed us by.

After dropping Cami and Lacy off at school, I took Luke to daily Mass each morning, and then three days a week left him at a Baptist preschool, where he was learning the cutest Christian songs and becoming a regular little preacher. When Luke prayed, it was with a childlike faith so dangerous and effective. Luke had decided he wanted a brother for Christmas and began praying for one. Pretty soon, he was telling everyone Jesus was bringing him a brother for Christmas.

"Where did that come from?" Scott asked.

I burst into tears because I really wanted a brother for Luke too.

Scott hugged me. "I make half of what I used to make at this job," he gently reminded me. "We don't have my flight pay anymore. We can't afford another kid."

"If God gives us a baby, he'll give us the money to pay for that baby." I wrapped my arms around my husband and held on tight.

I stopped shopping at the mall and my favorite store, Nordstrom's. I discovered thrift stores and bought used sleeping bags for the kids. We began camping, an inexpensive way to have fun. I also started getting our clothes at the secondhand stores. If one of the kids needed a new pair of shoes or a certain type of outfit, I prayed for God to provide it, and then made my rounds at the thrift stores I had discovered in our area.

Not once did God let me down. Everything we needed, he provided. And it was nice stuff at an incredible price. He was being so good to us.

Luke's red-haired baby brother was born on December 23rd, the same year Luke prayed for a brother to be delivered. I came home from the hospital on Christmas Eve, the day our family always opened gifts. We put John under the Christmas tree with a note on his baby blue basket—yes, the basket I won at church years earlier.

It read: *Here is your brother from Jesus.*

Merry Christmas, Luke.

Just one more prayer answered in a season of new beginnings.

Chapter Nineteen

> The two most important days in your
> life are the day you are born,
> and the day you find out why."
> — Mark Twain

For as long as I could remember night terrors had plagued me. Sometimes it felt like evil was trying to lift me off the bed while I was sleeping. Other times I felt paralyzed, like something sinister was upon me, holding me down, and I couldn't move. Vivid nightmares accompanied these unearthly sensations.

When I finally wrestled myself out of the nightmares and opened my eyes, a familiar dark figure stood in our bedroom. Air from the grave swirled around it. *You are mine,* it would convey, and intuitively I knew somewhere down the line an unholy pact had been made. This familiar spirit seemed inherited, and along with it came the ability to dream events that would later happen. Had the desire been there, I would have made a really good witch, but I didn't want to be a witch. I wanted to follow Christ.

Before I was saved, I accepted this torment of night terrors. Like somehow it was my heritage to have terrible dreams that didn't immediately disappear when I woke up. I went to a priest and asked him if the devil could bother me this way.

"Evil is just an idea man has created," the priest said. "You should see a therapist for these night terrors."

I didn't believe him. So, I sought out another priest. "I'm having nightmares," I told the second priest. "I've had them all my life. Now that I'm born again and love Jesus, when I wake up from these nightmares, a dark figure is standing there by the bed. It won't leave me alone. It's so frightening."

"The devil isn't real. You're seeing things," said the priest. "You need a psychiatrist."

I left that priest's office so disheartened and began to question my own sanity. After returning home and sitting with the Lord for a while, praying about it, I called my friend, Patsy, who had been a Christian all her life. I told her about my nightmares, and she said, "You need to go visit my pastor. Here is my church's phone number. Call and make an appointment with him. Pastor Gary has just returned from being a missionary in Africa. He can help you."

So I called Patsy's church. We were still living in that funky little rental house in Davis. A couple days later, in the middle of a big thunderstorm, I drove an hour north through farm fields darkened by ominous clouds to see Pastor Gary Moore, leader of Yuba City's Church of the Nazarene.

Yuba City was actually where I was born. Where my grandparents had their peach farm. Where I'd graduated high school. Storm clouds besieged the horizon as I neared my hometown. Thunder rolled. Lightning flashed. Rain pounded my windshield. It didn't feel like California. It felt like the Midwest with tornadoes on the way.

Pastor Gary was a quiet man with a peaceful office and a picture of his family on his desk. Along with three grown kids, he had a petite blonde wife with such a sweet face. I stared at the wife for a moment. You could just tell she was a beautiful person. At this point, I'd decided I was either crazy or the devil was after me. I wasn't sure which scared me more. I tentatively told Pastor Gary about my nightmares and the dark figure that sometimes wouldn't leave our bedroom at night. If he told me to go see a therapist like the priests, I was going to go. Maybe I was crazy.

I did most of the talking, sharing with him that this dark figure had always been in my life. Since I was a little girl, it had plagued me. Before I got saved, I would rub my eyes and the dark figure would almost always disappear after I woke up. I could still feel that unearthly cold swirling in the room, but that would slowly go away. Now that I was a Christian, rubbing my eyes didn't make the dark figure go away. It was tormenting me. I now slept with a candle burning in my bedroom, one of those Catholic Church votive candles with the Sacred Heart of Jesus on it.

Scott ignored my Jesus candle. Just like he ignored when I lay face down on the floor in total surrender to Christ. "Just step over your mom and leave her alone when she's like this," he'd tell the kids. "She'll snap out of it. She's just going through a religious phase. It'll pass."

I'm sure Scott was hoping if he ignored all this long enough, I'd quit disturbing him with my newly found religion, though both of us knew this is what had saved our marriage.

"You're experiencing spiritual warfare," Pastor Gary said when I finished telling him what I was struggling with. "In Africa we see more of that stuff than here in America. You need to learn who you are in Christ. Memorize Bible verses. He who is in you is greater than he who is in the world. Pray out loud in the name of Jesus when you wake from your nightmares."

I nodded my head and tears ran down my face. I was so relieved he didn't tell me to see a shrink or get some medication because I was nuts. After explaining more to me about the spiritual realm and the power of Jesus' name, he prayed for me. It was a beautiful prayer of deliverance.

When I left the church, I looked up into the sky. Ominous black thunderclouds rolled overhead as I walked to my car thanking the Lord for that meeting. I'd driven into the storm to get here. Now heading home on the backroads between Yuba City and Davis, I drove away from the thunder, lightning, and rain into a sparkling sunset sinking into freshly washed farm fields.

When I got home, I told Scott the good news. "I'm not crazy. But the bad news is we have a demon."

Scott's eyes widened. "Is this what that pastor told you?"

"Pretty much."

"What was the pastor like?"

"He was really nice. Pastor Gary lived in Africa most of his adult life as a missionary. He says there's more spiritual warfare in that country because people believe in demons there. Here, most people don't think the devil's legions are real and operating on this earth Do you believe in demons?" I asked my wide-eyed husband.

"I want to hear what that pastor has to say. Let's go to his church this Sunday."

Now my eyes widened. "I'm Catholic. I don't want to go to a Protestant Church."

"Well, we're going." Scott walked away without answering me about demons.

The good news of the Gospel slowly but surely began to change Scott once we started attending that Nazarene church on the outskirts of Yuba City. I continued to go to daily Mass, dragging three-year-old Luke along dressed like Lane Frost from the movie, *Eight Seconds*.

I called Luke our little cowboy preacher because he was always singing his Baptist Bible songs and he even slept in his cowboy gear. We grew to love the Nazarene church and decided to buy a house in Yuba City to be closer to it and my parents' farm in the Sutter Buttes. Scott would continue to commute to his ROTC teaching job in Davis until he finished getting a high school teaching credential by going to night school. He was leaving the Army and we began to dream about finding our own farm. We spent nearly all our weekends up at my parents', riding our horses all over the Buttes, and helping Dad with his cattle and Mom with her chickens, and all of us working on fences together.

About a year after we moved into our new house in Yuba City, Scott said, "I either have to believe what Pastor Gary is saying on Sundays or stop going to church."

Scott loved Pastor Gary. I would often find him after church talking with Pastor about his sermons. A few more months went by, and then, the week before Easter, the demon began to fill my nights again, even though I prayed out loud and used the name of Jesus when it came to our bedroom. The demon would leave when I ordered it in the name of Jesus to go but then come back the next night. I knew a massive battle was going on for Scott's soul. I was praying so hard the next night for Scott to be saved and the demon to leave that I began to pray in a different language.

It felt like I was praying in blood.

Jesus' blood.

Words I'd never heard before began to whisper out of my mouth as I prayed, something I'd never really been exposed to in either the Catholic Church or the Nazarene assembly. I'd never wanted to speak in tongues, as I knew it was called. That kind of thing freaked me out. But I felt the Spirit of God come upon me and this new language rolled out in desperate prayer.

Scott woke up and tried to wake me up too. He shook me, thinking I was having a nightmare.

"I'm awake," I said. "I'm praying."

"What the hell are you praying?" Scott grew angry fast.

"I think it's tongues."

Scott jumped out of the bed. "I've had enough! You've lost it! I'm calling Pastor Gary," he said, standing there nude beside the bed.

"Great, call him! I'm not crazy! The demon won't leave me alone. It's because of you! You need to accept Jesus!"

At least I was wearing pajamas. Scott looked so funny naked and furious, but it wasn't a funny moment. Really, it was quite frightening. Both of us were yelling now. Our argument woke up the kids. They came into our bedroom all afraid, like lost little lambs without their shepherd. Both Scott and I calmed down to comfort our children. Cami carried in John, a baby at the time, and I nursed him while Scott got dressed and took the three older kids back to their beds. I don't know what he told the kids, but I knew he was still so mad at me.

While nursing John, I quietly prayed in my new language. I was talking to God, and though I didn't know what I was saying, I could tell it was strengthening me in this fight for my husband's soul.

We went to see Pastor Gary hours later that morning. I let Scott do most of the talking.

"Paula was praying in a strange language last night. She keeps having nightmares and says a demon won't leave our house. There have been some strange noises and pictures falling off the wall for no reason. Things are getting weird." Scott sat back in his chair, looking a bit defeated.

That surprised me. Scott was not into weirdness. He did his best to explain away all strange things. But he couldn't explain what was happening in our home. Scott and I were both really upset. And tired.

Pastor Gary explained to us about the spiritual realm and the speaking of tongues. He was very patient. Very kind. We were so grateful for his calm, fatherly guidance. More freaky things happened that day, but by that very same night, Scott accepted Jesus as his savior.

Belief hit him at our kitchen table.

We'd picked up Scott's ninety-year-old grandpa at the airport that evening, and after I made dinner and cleaned up, I fell into bed beyond exhausted. I no longer sensed the demon in the house. It was easy to sleep.

Scott stayed up talking with his grandpa who'd flown in from Maine. Scott's great-grandpa, his grandpa's father, was a missionary in Sri Lanka, but Scott's grandpa had been a university professor in New York, and his views on religion were open to all beliefs. He was very educated.

"Do you think Jesus was the Son of God?" Scott asked his grandpa as they sat together late into the night talking at the kitchen table.

"I think he was a wise man, a good teacher," said Scott's grandpa.

At that moment, Scott said he knew with every fiber of his being that Jesus was the Son of God. The fear of the Lord overwhelmed Scott, and he told his grandpa they needed to go to bed.

In bed, where I was finally dead asleep, Scott stayed up all night repenting of his sins. He said he had a long list to confess. When he told me this the next morning, his face shining like I'd never seen before, I laughed and then I cried. We hugged each other, holding on tight for a long time, and in tears, we thanked Jesus for saving us and asked him to save our children too.

We were baptized together shortly after Easter, after Scott's grandpa flew home to Maine, and just before Scott was sent to a military school in Virginia. When he arrived at his hotel, Scott knew he was in trouble. A Hooter's restaurant shared the parking lot with the hotel, which excited the soldiers attending the school with Scott. When Scott turned on the television in his hotel room, porn played. He flipped the channel and tried to ignore the sex station, but temptation overwhelmed him to return to it.

Before becoming a Christian, porn was a regular part of Scott's life. But now, he had vowed to give it up. To hold tight to his Bible instead of sexual sin.

"I began to sweat," he told me over the phone that night, "Sitting there trying to watch the news with that free porn available. I thought about you, and I thought about Jesus, and I got out my Bible and tried to read Scripture, but, man, I wanted to watch that porn."

"What did you do?" I sat in a chair, nursing John, with the phone pressed to my ear.

"I walked out into the hallway, threw the key inside the room, and shut the door so I couldn't turn the porn back on. I went down to the front desk and told them I had free porn in my room. The lady told me it was on in my room because someone had already paid for it. She grinned and said, 'Go enjoy yourself.'

I told her that I really needed that cable box out of my room."

Two more hotel registration clerks came over and joined in the discussion about the free porn. They laughed among themselves, but Scott said he was insistent about having the box taken out of his room.

Another hotel employee turned around and laughed with the two registration girls as my poor husband said he stood there at the front desk sweating like a dog.

I wanted to tell Scott that dogs don't sweat. They pant to cool off, but he was so distraught sharing his story that I didn't try to interrupt him. You've got to understand, Scott is a manly man—a big, strong guy who sweats when he works out but never loses his cool in other situations. He's a pilot with nerves of steel. But porn was bringing him to his knees that night. He finished telling me his story with his voice low and taut with desperation.

"I returned to my room and stood in front of my locked door. I waited for I don't know how long for that repair guy to show up."

"Why are you standing out here in the hallway?" the repairman asked Scott when he arrived.

"I need you to get that free porn out of my room." Scott's heart pounded wildly. He knew he was in a battle he couldn't win without Jesus.

"You got free porn in your room?" The repairman pulled out a key card and opened the door.

"Yes, and I really need you to fix it for me," Scott said as he followed the repairman into the room.

The repairman turned on the TV, flipped through the channels to find the porn station, then stood there watching it. "Yep, you got yourself some free porn," the guy said with a grin on his face. He kept watching the porn.

"I wanted to punch him. I wanted to break the TV. I wanted to break my sin," Scott told me. I could hear the battle raging in his voice. In his mind. In his heart.

"I'm so sorry, babe. The devil set a trap for you because you just got baptized," I said, staring down at our baby, hardly believing how Scott was changing. How our marriage was changing in such a wondrous way.

"I'm no saint," said Scott. "Standing there with the repair guy, I watched that porn for a few more minutes. Then I told the guy if he didn't remove the box, I was going to rip it from the wall and throw it out the window." The repairman quickly unhooked the box and left.

But the temptation wasn't over. Every night of that deployment, the soldiers went to Hooters for dinner. Scott took a walk with a new Christian friend he'd made at the school to find food served by waitresses wearing modest clothes.

Now that's a miracle.

My husband hasn't viewed porn since that night in the hotel room. His only sexual gratification is me now.

I realize that this might be an awkward subject for some. It's kind of uncomfortable for me too, but can I just explain what happens when a wife becomes the only naked woman her husband ever sees? It's kind of like seeing a unicorn. Chasing a unicorn. Really wanting to catch that unicorn.

Chapter Twenty

So God Made a Farmer…
— Paul Harvey

Scott had left the Army to become a high school history teacher. I'd settled into being a stay-at-home mom, driving our oldest kids to three different soccer practices every day with John riding along in his car seat. After praying for several years for God to give us our own farm, we found the perfect property at the base of the Sutter Buttes three miles from the Sacramento River. It was an old almond orchard that had been abandoned for a long time. The trees were older than we were and the orchard grass hip high. A herd of deer lived in this ancient orchard along with thousands of valley quail that burst into flight when we got too close to their covey. My family bought the sixty acres of old almonds, and Scott and I were gifted twenty acres of it along the deep ravine that ran like a river during the winter rains. An old blue tractor came with the property.

My brother Patrick took the twenty acres beside us with the big oak tree, and my parents, their marriage in a good place now after years of trying to kill each other, claimed the twenty acres that bordered Patrick's property along the old county road. We all agreed to farm the land together. We sold our Yuba City house and were blessed to walk away from that new subdivision, just a couple years later, doubling our money. We gave all the money to my dad, who was through his midlife crisis and now deeply committed to our family. Dad drew the plans up for our two-story house with lots of windows that look out over our fields, and had it built for us. It's where my little fox lived with her four little kits before they grew up and made their way out into the big world beyond our farm.

I can't tell you how happy we were that first spring on our new farm, Scott out there on the old blue tractor. We nicknamed the tractor the Bluehawk and teased Scott about flying it, since he was no longer a Blackhawk helicopter pilot. Scott built fence around the property, with me and my big pregnant belly sitting on a blanket with eighteen-month-old John under the shade of an ancient almond tree in full bloom and the air perfumed with the scent of blossoms. Cami, Lacy, and Luke climbed the old almond trees, picking the blooms, and throwing them at each other. They all looked so cute with white petals in their hair.

A couple years later, after we built a chicken house near the horse corral, my mom bought us a bunch of baby chicks at the feed store and raised them for us so we could have fresh eggs. Our family needed all the help we could get, considering we had put every last dollar we had into our new farm and now had five kids. Joseph, we called him Joey, was born a year before we moved into our finished home. Joey and John quickly became best friends and partners in the mud. They knew nothing but the farm and were always covered in dirt. Neither liked to wear shirts or shoes so I gave up and let them run around like half-dressed hillbillies.

As our first batch of chickens matured that year, a black rooster in the mix grew big and mean. We tolerated that awful rooster for a few more years, until John, a kindergartener around this time, had had enough. John watched *Kung Fu Panda* each day and practiced his karate skills. That mean old rooster had gotten the better of him and his brothers one too many times. Even big brother Luke was afraid of the rooster. Poor Joey—all of three years old with curly blond hair and bright blue eyes—got attacked by the rooster the week before, and John was ready to do something about it. Nobody messed with Joey. John was his protector.

"I'm not scared of that mean old rooster," John told me as we cracked eggs together into a frying pan that morning as the sun streamed through the kitchen windows. "I know kung fu, and I'm gonna teach that big, bad bird a lesson!"

"That rooster is as tall as you. He could peck your eyes out," I informed John, being the protective mother that I am.

"He's gonna peck the bottom of my shoe when I kick him in the beak," John replied, full of redheaded sass.

John was small for his age, his dark blue eyes shining with grit and determination. He looked so much like my brother Patrick, and acted so serious about taking on the rooster. I tried not to laugh at him while scrambling eggs. I knew John was as frightened of that old rooster as the rest of us. When I fed the chickens,

I took a broom along. That big black rooster flew at you with his spurs out. A smack with the broom did the trick, but you had to be fast. He'd give you the chicken-eye, and he'd come bullying you right out of his pen.

I hated that rooster.

After breakfast John went to school, and later that day, my mom—Oma to her grandkids—picked him up from kindergarten at his noon dismissal. Before coming to the house, they stopped to feed the chickens and gather the eggs. Oma took her sweet time getting out of the car as John ran ahead to the chicken coop. A moment later John was screaming bloody murder.

Oma ran as fast as grandmas can to find John sprawled on his back with the rooster on top of him in the chicken pen. That bird was spurring and pecking and flapping his big black wings in John's face. Oma jumped in and kicked that old rooster across the pen and back while peeing her pants in the process (literally), screaming along with John.

Of course, Oma won that battle.

Oma wins every battle.

After his run-in with the rooster, John came into the house and collapsed in my arms.

"That old rooster about pecked my eyes out!" John was crying so hard I could barely understand him.

"If you don't find a pair of pants that fit me, I'm going home." Oma huffed into my laundry room, where I sat on the floor holding John in my lap. "Your son and that rooster nearly gave me a heart attack! My pants are soaked. I'm going to put that rooster in a stew pot!"

Farming Grace

I'd been folding clothes when the two arrived all upset over the rooster. I washed the scratches on John's neck, dabbed them with medicine, and then found some sweats for Oma to wear. My mom's taller than me, which isn't saying much since Oma's not very big, though to me, she's always been larger than life. We also call Oma "the General" because Dad dubbed her that years ago when she was bossing him around. Oma bosses everyone around.

I handed Oma sweats that belonged to Cami, but I never let Cami wear them out of the house because of the word "Juicy" embellished across the rear end. I didn't want men reading my teenage daughter's backside, so she only got to wear the sweats at home.

An hour later, Oma was mopping my kitchen floor with *Juicy* shouting from her backside. I had to walk away, swallowing my laughter. Had I laughed at her, Oma would have hit me with the mop.

Chapter Twenty-One

> There is something about the outside of a
> horse that is good for the inside of a man.
> — Winston Churchill

When I was growing up, Dad took care of Patrick and me. On weekends he took us to work with him. Dad was always working, either at his engineering firm, or around the farm, or helping a friend build a house or a barn or whatever. Patrick and I had to work too. The first hammer I tried to pick up was bigger than me. I remember Mom sleeping most days with a fan on in her bedroom before she left for her night shift at the hospital. Out in the living room with Dad after dark, we had to be real quiet watching TV. It wasn't hard; I loved my dad and wanted to be a good girl for him.

I stayed quiet.

Dad's hair was thick and dark, his eyes sky blue. When he laughed, it sounded like a song sung by a happy person, but Dad wasn't always happy. When I was little, money was tight, and Dad and Mom started from scratch after clawing their way through college together. None of my grandparents went to college. My parents were self-made. This is what people said about starting out poor and finishing well-off: you're self-made.

Dad couldn't always afford the whiskey he favored or the tobacco he chewed or the skinny, little cigarettes he rolled himself while watching TV. I loved helping him roll those little cigarettes while *Mutual of Omaha's Wild Kingdom* played on television. It came on before Walt Disney on Sunday nights. We never missed those two shows. They were our favorites.

Dad taught me how to make highballs, potato soup, and shotgun shells. During hunting season, he disappeared off to the duck blinds out in the wetlands or up to the mountains after big bucks. One night in the middle of a lightning storm, Dad and I crawled around our green 1970s shag carpet together unplugging lamps, the television, and anything else connected to the wall. Thunder shook the house, but it never crossed my mind we might be in danger.

I was with my dad.

He never told me I was pretty or said "I love you" when I was young, yet I always knew he found me special. I thought he was special too. Both of us were hardheaded and determined to have our own way.

In junior high I pined for a pair of brand-name platform heels that cost way too much. Without fanfare, Dad bought them for me, as well as a Toyota Celica with a sunroof when I turned sixteen.

These things didn't come easy. Everyone worked hard in our family to make a living. Dad grew up poor and went barefoot in the summer along with his brothers. He stocked shelves in a grocery store while going to high school and also put himself through college to become a civil engineer. Sometimes he'd bring home a horse or a cow instead of payment for his engineering work.

"Lots of people lead hard lives. You gotta help folks when you can," he'd say.

We've had our ups and downs—roaring fights and quiet talks. Taking horses to the high country with our fishing poles will forever be my favorite thing, along with Dad's campfire meals mad with onions. In the valley, I couldn't stand the smell of an onion, but in the mountains with him I couldn't imagine that cast-iron pan without them.

Now that I'm older, I still wrestle with what to get Dad for Father's Day.

"Don't buy him a shirt; he has plenty," Mom tells me each year. But in the end, a shirt it is, along with Swedish fish candy because I can't think of anything else unless Wilbur Smith has a new novel out. Everything he wants, he goes and buys for himself. This isn't hard since his wants are few. He wears out his cowboy boots in which he tucks his reading glasses from Walmart. The Dodge diesel pickup he drives has more than 300,000 miles. I've heard him cuss in church, but he keeps a picture of Jesus on his truck's dash, along with the gas card he shares with me. Often, he pays for the oil my old Suburban burns like kindling wood.

Dad isn't perfect, but he has a perfect Savior. I'm not sure how well he knows Jesus, but I've given up beating him over the head with my Bible. This has only worn me out and put distance between us. Knowing God's law and living God's grace are two different things. Slowly, I'm learning. I have to say I've seen more old-fashioned integrity in Dad's life than a lot of Christians I know. He's never dressed up himself or his sins. He likes his beer but doesn't get drunk and go wild like he did when I was younger. At least not very often anymore.

Dad's what-you-see-is-what-you-get philosophy has helped me tremendously in my walk with God. Honesty does far more for the soul than getting all pretty for church.

My dad may be many things, but a hypocrite has never been one of them.

Getting all pretty had overtaken my life by the time I hit my thirties. I no longer recognized myself in the mirror. My hair was bleached blond. My makeup too heavy. Breast implants had changed my slim figure. I'd lost all youthful beauty in my life. Where had it gone? I could hardly remember what my own beauty looked like, but I knew I could find it on the back of the right horse.

"He spins on a dime," the woman who sold me Soda Pop said the day I bought him. I'd gone to look at this horse listed in the newspaper. "I've raced him a few times, and he's super fast, but he's too sensitive for racing. Down in Mexico they beat him up real bad. See his scars? He needs a good home with a little gal like you riding him," said the woman.

I saw the tale of abuse on Soda's face: scars around his mouth, across his forehead where the hair no longer grew due to wounds healed there. Often this happens to horses if they get a bad cut or gash—they lose the hair in that spot. And if the hair ever does come back, it grows in white. Soda had a lot of white spots. Still, he was beautiful—a bay quarter horse gelding, all muscle, bone, and bright brown eyes looking me over in return. That's the thing about owning a horse. In a way, that horse owns you. If I bought Soda, we'd be in this together.

And the thing I was after was beauty.

I was sick of plastic pretty. I wanted beauty back. I was thirty-one years old with three kids, a two-story house in the suburbs, and an SUV that hit every soccer game, school event, and military function. This was before we had more kids and moved to our farm. Before I returned to my faith. I was searching for myself. I thought a good horse was the answer.

The first time I rode Soda Pop, he scared me to death in a walnut orchard. After that, for months, my knees would shake when I stepped into the saddle. If a cow was around, Soda would hunker down like a dog, then that spinning-on-a-dime thing the gal warned me about would happen. I wore sports bras and prayed a lot. It's a miracle I never landed in the dirt.

If I could sum up beauty in one story, it would be facing Dad's bull. The bull had gone on a walkabout looking for greener pastures. Greener, meaning more cows to breed. Dad, Scott, and I went after that bad old bull—Dad on a four-wheeler, Scott on Duke—a rawboned buckskin gelding—and me on Soda Pop.

Way up in the Sutter Buttes we rode to get that old bull—up to where the wild things are in the crags and rocks and twisted oak trees of the smallest mountain range in the world. The wildest thing that day in the Buttes was Dad's old bull. Two thousand pounds of raging hormones. That bull wasn't about to leave a bunch of dairy cows he'd found way up in the Buttes. A place called Peace Valley that wasn't peaceful that day. When Soda Pop and I cut open the herd of black-and-white Holsteins, Dad's bull looked us in the eye and put his head down, which is never a good sign in a large animal. Dad's bull shook his big black skull from side to side as if to say, "No way. I'm not going with you."

Soda Pop was shaking. I was shaking. The bull pawed the ground. Dad roared up, gassing his four-wheeler, making the bull really mad. Scott and I began moving the bull's girlfriends—those dairy cows were comedians. I could almost hear them saying, "Oh my gosh, I broke a hoof! Stop herding me. You made me swallow my cud!"

Soda must have been thinking, *You've got to be kidding me. You call these cows? They're Broadway actresses in disguise.*

Soda grew so disgusted with the Holsteins, he began biting the slow-moving girls on their butts. I held on and let Soda do his thing. He was the Mexican rodeo horse again—a real cowboy's horse. And on his back, I was a woman in search of beauty. The girl I'd lost by pursuing the looks you could purchase through surgery, designer clothes, and expensive makeup.

It took us all afternoon, but we finally got the herd to Dad's fence line. The bull wasn't happy about it, but we hadn't tried to take him away from the heifers, so that kept him calm enough to get him down from the mountains. At the fence, it was time to split the bull away from the Holsteins. That's when this monster of an animal showed his stuff, charging at Dad on the motorbike. Dad gassed the bike back at the bull. Instead of a collision, the bull spun at the last minute and tore like a freight train toward the heart of the Buttes.

Scott spurred Duke after him. The bull rounded on Scott and Duke. Duke reared sideways when the bull came at him. He and Scott hit a ravine and crashed down. Scott went flying in a spray of mud. Duke rolled into the ravine. Dad raced to rescue Scott, heading off the bull that was charging after my husband on the ground. But, again, the bull made a dash for freedom, and Dad opened his four-wheeler to full speed. The bull jumped the twisting ravine, and Dad tried to jump it too, but was unable to clear it.

The four-wheeler hurtled into the side of the deep ditch. Dad went flying like a rag doll. In the process of racing Soda Pop to Scott's side, I screamed in horror.

I thought Dad was dead.

"I'm okay! Check on your dad!" Scott yelled to me.

I galloped Soda Pop over to Dad.

"Get the bull!" Dad yelled from where he sprawled in the dirt, cussing a blue streak.

Soda Pop was all for it. He knew the bull was the real target and was delighted to be done with those silly dairy cows. I grabbed the saddle horn and prayed as Soda ran for all his worth to cut the bull off. In a beautiful act of horsemanship, Soda did all the work. I did nothing but hang on for dear life as Soda turned the bull back to the fence and pushed two thousand pounds of fury through the gate. I jumped off Soda to close the gate in case the bull doubled back. Scott rode up, and Dad arrived on his broken motorbike.

About this time, we noticed the bull trotting around Dad's pond—a decent size lake, really.

"He's going to jump the fence on the other side," Dad said. He turned the limping motorbike around to try to head off the bull. But there was no way the broken motorbike could make it to the other side of the sprawling pond in time. The only chance to stop the bull was to swim the lake.

Soda must have been thinking the same thing. As soon as I leaped onto his back, he ran like the wind for the pond. We plowed into the water. The bull ran faster around the lake. Soda swam hard. As I rode, clinging to his back, freezing water washed over my shoulders. It was wintertime. We reached the other side at the corner of the fence seconds before the bull arrived there. He was bottlenecked by another fence and the pond now.

Soda Pop stood his ground, both of us trembling.

It could have been the cold water or the adrenaline of the chase, but when you are face-to-face with a raging bull, it can really give you the shakes.

It seemed like forever but was probably a few seconds that Soda and I squared off with the bull. Because of the two fences and the pond, the bull would have to go over the top of us to escape into the Buttes. Believe me, that old bull thought about it. I could see it in his eyes.

Water and sweat poured off Soda Pop. I may have sweated too, though it was forty degrees out.

Please, God, turn this bull around.

The bull gave a furious shake of his head, snot flying from his nostrils, then spun sideways and jumped the fence into Dad's other pasture.

A minute later, it seemed miraculous that Dad arrived on that side of the fence with a huge stick in his hand. He waved the bull toward his own herd. Fortunately, Dad's herd was in that pasture, and when the bull saw all his old wives, he willingly rejoined them.

Talk about a thing of beauty. A ride of faith. Dusk appeared on the horizon like the credits of a movie. A meadowlark sang out as twilight broke over the farm. Winter moves this way in the Sutter Buttes, afternoon abruptly turning to evening.

Soda Pop and I rode toward Scott, who was riding toward us with a look of wonder on his face.

"You're so beautiful. I think you have pond moss in your hair. Can I marry you all over again?" Scott said as if seeing me for the very first time.

"I'm a mess," I said, realizing how drenched and disheveled I was.

"Are you kidding? You look like the girl I fell in love with." Scott couldn't stop grinning. "I see that little red-haired girl who tackled the calf when we were teenagers."

While riding our horses back to the barn, Scott told me about the moment he knew I was the one for him. I'd invited him to the farm to help us work cattle. He was a college football player, and when we began to brand the calves, it never crossed my mind that Scott wouldn't jump right in, holding the calves down alongside me. When I tackled that first calf in the working corral, I expected my big, muscular boyfriend to jump in and help.

Scott just stood there dumbstruck staring at me and the calf.

On the ground in the mud, I held the bawling calf down long enough for Dad to land the L/ brand he burns onto all his cattle. The smell of scorched flesh filled my senses. Smoke from the branding iron blinded me. The calf kicked me and pooped on me, and I couldn't believe Scott just watched the whole thing. Any country boy with a lick of sense would have joined in, but Scott was too taken aback by it all.

"You should have seen your momma," Scott tells the kids about once a year. "When I saw her take down that calf, I knew she had to have my babies. Your mom had cow crap all over her and didn't even care. She was so beautiful. I loved her right then."

Chapter Twenty-Two

> Our scars make us know that
> our past was for real.
> — Jane Austen

Soda Pop got really sick from a mosquito bite. We did all we could; Dad and Mom even had the vet come out to look at him. I think this was the first animal they really tried to save for me. When Dad ran over my dog, Gidget, when I was in high school, he went and got his gun. I didn't even get to say goodbye. He shot Gidget, and that was that. I'd had her since I was nine years old, and I can't tell you how much losing my little dog that way hurt me.

Dad wanted to shoot Soda too. He told me Soda Pop was in bad shape, but he still promised not to shoot him. I had a bad feeling that day, so I drove to the farm and got there just in time to meet Dad at the barn with his deer rifle.

"Get out of here," Dad yelled at me, cussing too—the F-word all over the place. "I gotta shoot your f—ing horse!"

Dad was shaking, and I was shaking.

"Please, Dad, let me say goodbye to Soda Pop first."

Dad lowered his gun, then went over and leaned on his pickup truck, waiting for me to do what I needed to do.

I knelt beside Soda's head. He'd made dust angels in the dirt trying to get up. In the shadow of the barn on that winter afternoon with the sun streaming down—my Pearl Harbor Day birthday had just passed—I felt so old. "You've been such a good horse," I whispered in Soda's ear. "Thank you for bringing beauty back into my life."

I pressed my face to Soda's cheek as my tears baptized him. Looking back, I see these were really God's tears. God knew how much Dad and I needed this moment to heal the past.

Soda was looking at me intently as I sang softly to him.

"Jesus loves us this I know, for the Bible tells me so. Little ones to him belong; they are weak, but he is strong. Yes, Jesus loves us. Yes, Jesus loves us, yes, Jesus loves us, the Bible tells me so."

Peace came over me after that lullaby, and I could see Soda had grown peaceful too. After trying so hard to get up, he now rested in the angel he had made, his eyes soft and growing sleepy. It was an uncommonly dry winter, and the dirt was like powder around Dad's barn. Maybe this was the beginning of the rains disappearing in California—with that terrible drought on the horizon that we didn't know about yet.

I kissed Soda on his velvet muzzle, told him I how much I loved him, then climbed over the fence to walk to Dad's truck.

Dad stood there cradling his rifle.

He looked so old.

Even now, in his seventies, Dad usually looks like a man just in his fifties. But that day, Dad looked as ancient as the craggy mountains—all rocky tops, deep valleys, and years of hard storms.

"I'm sorry I gotta shoot your horse." Dad looked me right in the eye. "Soda's been a damn good horse for you."

"I know." I hugged Dad. His bones felt frail under my hands, like bird bones. Dad's body had never felt fragile to me in my life. But that day it did.

"I won't shoot him till you drive away," Dad promised.

I nodded, tears splashing down my cheeks. Then, I walked to my SUV while the other horses stood around like scared kids. I had to shoo them away in order to get behind the wheel and head down the hill.

As I drove out the farm's gate with the big crossbeam overhead with a horse and bull skulls nailed to it—Dad's idea of warning people from entering the property—I switched on my radio. I was crying but still enfolded within God's peace. One of my favorite songs, "Blessed Be Your Name," flowed out of my radio. "You give and take away…."

I learned the sacrifice of praise that day. I didn't want to praise God as Dad was back at the barn putting Soda down, but I did. I rolled down the window and began to sing along with the song, softly at first, then louder and louder until I was hollering the song with my heart breaking. God was there with Dad and Soda at the barn. And there with me on this twisting country road winding through almond orchards with the sun shining through the trees.

Do we ever escape our childhoods?

Do the painful memories ever really let us go?

I didn't dwell on Dad's shooting Soda Pop the way I had on the deaths of so many of the animals I loved when I was little. I put a tight lid on this fresh trauma and moved on. Maybe I was done riding horses. I couldn't imagine replacing Soda Pop with another horse. I didn't have to think. I just needed to drive home and hug my kids. My husband. Only my horse had died.

The horse God had given to bring beauty back to me.

I forced myself to keep singing along with the radio. "You give and take away... blessed be your name ...."

After Soda Pop was gone, his empty pasture made my heart ache. My little fox's den was in the middle of Soda's field with the old almond trees. The almonds blew down in a fierce storm the same week I gave birth to Garry James, our sixth child, the year after Soda died. When I came home from the hospital with baby Garry, it looked as if a massive tornado had roared across our farm. The storm seemed fitting, since my sixth pregnancy was a storm as well.

I was thirty-nine years old when this pregnancy took us by surprise.

"How did this happen?" Scott asked when I shared the startling news that I was knocked up. *Again.*

"You tell me," I answered. "I'm not the one shooting live rounds down range." Something Scott says all the time about making babies.

"We were careful." Scott furiously toweled off from his shower, as if he was in a hurry for no reason that morning. The alarm on his face almost made me laugh. I hadn't wanted to be pregnant. This baby was due a few months after I would turn forty. But there we were, two middle-aged people standing in the bathroom staring at each other in shock. Four months later, we were even more shocked.

"Your baby has cysts in his brain," the doctor informed us after a routine ultrasound at twenty weeks. "We want to send you to Sacramento for further testing." He talked on about Down syndrome and our choices, and everything became sharp and jagged in my head and in my heart. The moment was crushing.

I already knew we weren't going to Sacramento for further testing. You can't change Down syndrome, and we couldn't afford testing anyway.

We went home, and I cried my eyes out. Then spent five months praying for a healthy baby. We asked everyone at our church to pray. We stood with Pastor Gary's hands on Scott's and my shoulders as I cradled my baby belly, tears streaming down my face.

"Please, Lord, we pray for this baby," said Pastor Gary. "Lord, we believe what you say. We believe this baby will be born healthy and strong and beautiful."

Pastor Gary's prayer surprised me. He was white-haired now and so wise, not a go-out-on-a-limb type of pastor. His confident prayer filled me with hope. Whatever happened, I now knew that this child would be named Garry. After my dad, Garry, and Pastor Gary, who had brought Scott to the Lord with all those faithful sermons preached each Sunday.

But the days dragged on all tangled by doubt and fear after that prayer. People approached us at church.

"Down syndrome babies are so special. This is such an amazing blessing for you," a number of Christian friends told me with great big smiles.

What I found so strange during that difficult pregnancy was that non-Christian friends did a better job comforting me than many of my Christian friends. My nonbelieving friends cried with me over this Down syndrome diagnosis. They didn't give me platitudes with a smile. If one more church friend told me a Down syndrome baby was a special blessing, I was ready to tell them, "Google it. Half of Down syndrome babies die in the womb. Many arrive with serious medical issues and die their first year. Those that thrive as babies rarely live past middle age. I'll be forty when I have this baby. Who will take care of him when I'm dead and gone? Our insurance is crap. This is gut-wrenching for us."

I spent half the pregnancy crying. Then, a month before my due date, my labor began early. The hospital tried to stop it, but that worked only for a week. Then a big storm hit, and we drove through a city without electricity to a hospital running on generators. But instead of letting me have the baby, they gave me another shot to stop my labor and sent me home.

Six hours later, we were speeding back to the hospital.

I was now in hard labor, afraid the baby would be born in our car.

After arriving at the hospital, our son came so fast, the nurse screamed for help. Someone found a midwife walking the hospital halls. They brought the midwife to my room just in time to watch the baby make a hasty entrance as my water erupted, spraying everyone in the room. I felt bad for the nurses and midwife. If another woman's amniotic fluid splashed all over me, I'd freak out. But nobody cared—until I started to bleed.

A nurse frantically put in an IV, pumping me full of Pitocin to stop my bleeding.

When it was finally over, and I got to see our baby, he looked perfectly healthy and absolutely beautiful. However, the next day we were informed he had a heart problem. They put little Garry in the NICU and brought in a pediatric cardiologist.

"Is this because he has Down syndrome?" Scott asked the cardiologist, a young Israeli doctor sporting a beret with a cup of Starbucks coffee in his hand.

"Who told you your son has Down syndrome? He does not have Down syndrome," the young doctor said adamantly. "We think he aspirated on his way out, and this has affected one of his heart valves. He should be all right eventually."

After a week in the NICU, we carried home the sweetest baby ever.

Garry James was uncommonly calm, incredibly bright-eyed, and unbelievably patient, which he needed since the pediatric cardiologist watched his heart for a year, making sure it healed properly. Every few weeks, and later, every few months, a nurse would strap on a halter monitor to check Garry James's heart activity. Baby Garry stared up at me with great trust while all those wires were attached to his chest with stickers until the doctor gave the "all clear."

But after Garry James's birth, our finances weren't all clear, and neither were our fields. The big storm had toppled all the old almond trees in our pasture. It looked as if a hurricane hit our farm. We were too tired to do anything about it. We also desperately needed money to pay our mounting medical bills. Scott thought about returning to flying for the income. We loved our little Christian school where Scott taught high school history, but his teaching salary was small. He could earn so much more as a pilot.

In desperation on a Sunday morning, we went to the altar at church to pray for God to provide for us. Later that afternoon, a white pickup truck with government license plates came down our driveway. The man parked beside our basketball hoop and walked to our front door.

"What are you going do with all these downed trees in your fields?" he asked Scott.

"Firewood, I guess." I could hear in Scott's voice how tired he was. We'd been through such a hard season, cutting up trees wasn't even on our radar.

"I'm with the State of California. Someone told me the trees we're looking for were here. We're making salmon nests in the Sacramento River. We want to buy all your downed trees."

When the guy left, Scott and I wept in each other's arms. A week later, the state sent us a check for nine thousand dollars and came in with a crane and an eighteen-wheeler truck to haul all the downed trees off our property. We paid bills and praised God for his provision.

The following spring we were fishing with Dad in his striper boat on the Sacramento River. The water was low enough for me to see our trees sticking out of the side of the levee into the river. The wood now provided nests for baby salmon to hide from the stripers that ate them. Our dead trees had become trees of life.

Chapter Twenty-Three

> I had rather be on my farm, than
> be emperor of the world.
> — George Washington

When we first bought our land, I ran my hands through the rich, dark soil like a girl who loves her hair, combing it with my fingers. Our soil is sandy loam, a deep silvery brown and thick with potassium. Considering that a lack of potassium almost killed me, I value a land that holds this mineral and hopefully delivers it into our fruit, nuts, and vegetable garden.

Sandy loam is considered the best topsoil. It keeps plants hydrated and yet drains well enough that air gets into the ground. My family didn't buy our land for this magnificent soil. We didn't even know it had magnificent soil. We bought it for the location and the breathtaking view. The Sutter Buttes rise right up in front of us, rolling hills with steep peaks that are green in the winter and golden in the summertime. Behind our farm, right down the road, runs the Sacramento River. It is this river that has left all this sandy loam soil for us. Before the levees were built, the river reached all the way to our farm during the rainy season.

When the rains taper off in the spring, swallows from the river come and drive us nuts. They try to nest around the eves of our house. Their favorite spot is right under our front door. I shoo these pretty little birds away with a broom, like an old woman determined to keep flying mice away. If I can outlast the swallows for about three days, they finally give up and go elsewhere.

Our pest man knocks their nests down year after year. Only one nest I don't let him touch. And I don't touch it either. It's on our back wall above my laundry room window. Swallows come back to where they were born, so the same little swallow family rebuilds in that spot under the eve every spring with mud from our orchard. I missed them with my broom their first year because I was pregnant and on bedrest, and we were between pest control companies. So, they established themselves, and now I don't have the heart to shoo them away. They take our sandy loam soil and make it their sandcastle home and raise their sweet little babies there. Year after year, their dedication astounds me.

I love that God has put something inside the swallows that brings them home no matter where they go. They fly far away, and then they come back to us.

Farming Grace

When Garry James was a year old, some dear friends, Steve and Bridget Isle, who raise quarter horses on a ranch south of Sacramento, called and said, "Bring your horse trailer down. We have a gift for you."

Because Steve is a colonel in the Army, and at one time was one of Scott's bosses, we did what he said. When we got to their house, Bridget led out a mare trailed by a new foal, a bay filly with a white heart on her forehead. Steve was beaming. "She's a sweetheart just like you, Paula," he said. "We know how devastated you were to lose Soda Pop. We are giving you this filly to take his place."

"Oh my gosh," I cried, and then I really cried, tears filling my eyes. "She's perfect! I love her! Thank you!" I hugged Steve and Bridget and they helped us load up the mare and foal.

"You can bring us back Hope when it's time to wean your girl," Bridget said. Hope had a crippled foot but was a pretty buckskin paint and a really good mom to her baby.

I named my filly Heart, and two years later, she went to the horse trainer. While she was in training, I returned to the skin doctor to have a spot checked on my leg. I'd developed a strange brown mole on my calf while pregnant with baby number seven. Yes, I said seven.

Scott was set on another child after Garry James was born, but it was the last thing I wanted. It took several trips to the altar at church where I prayed, begged, cried, and pleaded with God to grant me the faith and obedience to have this last baby in my forties.

My dear friend Kay assured me there was only a two percent chance of getting pregnant in my forties. I always listen to Kay.

She gives such good advice, and I usually feel at peace after talking and praying with her. Two percent sounded like pretty good odds to me. But a month later, I informed Kay, "I am the two percent." Then I laughed and cried. Really cried because I'd spent half my adult life pregnant and wasn't even good at it.

About a year before this last pregnancy, I woke up with a partially deflated tire. That's what one of my breasts looked like in the mirror. Our insurance was terrible at the time. I knew it wouldn't cover having my implants removed. I made an appointment with the plastic surgeon in Sacramento who'd put them in eight years earlier, determined to have him fix my problem in his office without anesthesia.

"We have really good new implants," he said when I went to my appointment.

"I want them removed," I answered point-blank.

He spent a few minutes trying to talk me out of it. Trying to convince me to upgrade my implants. "Our new ones are really good. You'll really like them," he encouraged me.

"Look," I said, "I'm forty-one years old. I don't care about implants anymore. Have you ever tried to ride a horse with implants in your chest? They're in the way." I thought of Soda Pop, and my heart ached.

"What about your husband? Doesn't he want you to have nice implants?"

"My husband loves me just the way I am. He supports me getting my implants removed." A painful lump arose in my throat. Scott was supportive of taking them out, but this was a risk. My breasts might look terrible afterward. What if Scott was less attracted to me?

"Well, let's schedule the surgery," said the doctor.

"That's the thing. I can't afford to have surgery. I want you to remove them here in your office without putting me to sleep."

The doctor's eyes widened. "This isn't a simple procedure." His gaze roved over my face and body, staring for a moment at my cross necklace. "You look healthy and strong, but—"

"I'm good," I said, interrupting him. "I've had six babies, five without epidurals. I grew up on a farm. I'm tough. My mom is a nurse. If we got hurt, she doctored us at home. I can handle this procedure. Will you please do it for me?"

A week later, I was back in his office without my shirt on. With my cross necklace resting on my breastbone, I thought the doctor would make me remove it or put it behind my back like he had while taking pictures of my breasts eight years earlier. But he didn't say a word about the necklace. I was more than glad to keep it on. I'd been praying for Jesus to get me through this procedure and the aftermath of it.

The doctor stuck needle after needle around my breasts to numb them. I lay there with my eyes closed, praying. The shots pinched, but I didn't move. I wanted this over and done with. I didn't want to be put to sleep. What if I died under anesthesia?

Vanity killed your mother, I imagined my children being told. The thought of expiring that way gave me the gumption to get it done wide awake. I could do it. God would get me through it. I was counting on the Lord to carry me that day.

"Are you doing okay?" the doctor asked as he yanked and pulled on the ruptured implant after cutting me open.

"I'm fine," I whispered, trying not to lose my concentration on Jesus.

"We should have put you to sleep. The implants are attached to your body. I'm going to have to really pull to get them out."

"Really pull," I insisted.

Jesus, help me. Help the doctor. By your wounds I am healed.

An hour later, it was over. My breasts were glued and bandaged. I sat on the curb waiting for my friend Kristin, a sweet pastor's wife, to pick me up. When she arrived, we prayed in her car.

"Oh, God, thank you for this new beginning in Paula's life," Kristin spoke over me. "Heal her body, and let her life glorify you." Kristin's soft voice was so soothing. So full of faith and assurance. Her prayer filled me with hope.

When my husband came through the door after work, he walked right over to me fixing dinner in the kitchen. "How did it go today?"

"Well, now I have two flat tires," I said. "I hope you still love me."

"I didn't marry you for your breasts." Scott gave me a mischievous grin. "I married you for your butt." He squeezed my rear end and then put his arms around me. "I'm so glad you're home, Babe. I love you. You're really cooking dinner tonight?"

"The kids are hungry. And you're hungry."

"I'm always hungry," Scott smiled. "For you."

He pulled me closer, careful not to touch my wounded chest, careful not to wipe the powder off my new wings. Like a weary little butterfly wrestling out of a tight plastic cocoon, I was finally freeing my true self. I felt battered, bruised, and brave all at once.

After having my implants removed, my breasts perked right up when I gained weight with pregnancy and produced milk like a dairy cow. I was grateful we didn't have to buy formula. Plus, I loved nursing my babies. I got to sit in a chair with nobody bothering me—*nobody but Daddy wants to see Mommy's breasts.* So, the kids left me alone for twenty minutes.

Our seventh child we named Cruz. His real name is Christian, but I've been calling him Cruz since I found out I was pregnant in the Santa Cruz Mountains during our family camp that summer. We actually named him Christian after the camp, Redwood Christian Park, as the name Redwood just didn't work for us, and also because we wanted this baby to be a Christian. Not surprisingly, Cruz is by far our most rebellious child yet.

His strong will exhausted me. Scott called him the terrorist. "He doesn't let you sleep. Doesn't let you eat. He holds you hostage night and day," said Scott.

"He's a toddler," I told Scott.

"He's a terrorist," Scott insisted.

Christian was barely weaned when the doctor biopsied the mole on my leg.

I will never forget the evening I got the call. It was five p.m. and I'd just pulled into our driveway.

"I'm sorry," said the doctor. "It's melanoma. We need to schedule you for surgery ASAP."

I caught my breath. "Okay," I said, my voice quivering. I nodded my head "yes" and then "no," tears splashing down my face as I gripped the steering wheel with the doctor rambling on about the treatment.

That night I held Cruz in my lap and silently cried into his soft brown curls. He wasn't even two years old yet. I didn't want to die and leave him and his brothers without a mom. The girls were away at college. Cami was married now and about ready to graduate as a speech therapist. Lacy was pressing into nursing school. Luke was a rebellious teenager wrecking cars and keeping me awake at night with worry. John, Joey, and Garry James were happy little boys. I did my best to hide my sadness and fear from them that night. Scott seemed a little shell-shocked. I don't remember him saying anything, only holding me when I sobbed in his arms after the boys were in bed.

My mom had survived a bout with melanoma in her thirties. She told me she had knelt beside her bed and asked the Lord to let her live to raise her children. So, I did this too. I knelt down and said the same prayer in the hallway between our bedroom and bathroom the following morning. I have no idea why I hit my knees in the hallway, but that's where I landed, begging God to let me live and then finally sobbing in acceptance if he took my life instead. I gave God all my dreams that day: riding Heart for the first time, finally becoming a published author, eventually becoming a grandma. My grandkids would call me Poppy. In college

I chose this name because my friend Rhonda insisted one night when we were drunk together that we choose our grandma names.

"I'm twenty years old. Why on earth would I choose a grandma name?"

"Just do it." Rhonda waved her cigarette in my face. "We are going to be the hottest damn grandmas on the planet. I'm going to be Nana."

When I chose the name Poppy, Rhonda laughed so hard, she burned herself with her cigarette. "Poppy?!" She all but yelled in my face. "What the hell is a Poppy?"

"Well, what the hell is a Nana? Is that like a nanny goat?"

"You b—!" Rhonda cried, "I ain't no nanny goat!"

I sat there in the hallway remembering this profanity-laced conversation while drunk in college and realized how blind and lost I once was. "I'm so sorry," I told God. "I haven't lived a very good life. But I am completely yours. In life or in death, your will be done."

Then I bargained a little. "If you let me live, I will do anything you ask. I will stop riding horses and work for you. I will serve you with all my heart, spreading the Gospel as best I can through writing, speaking, and evangelizing. And I will raise my children to love you, I swear I will." Then I sobbed into my hands with my back against the wall.

I first found my courage on the back of a pony. The adults in my life believed in horses and placed me on a pony before I could walk to get me out of the way at my grandparents' horse stables. Ponies were my first babysitters.

These tiny, stubborn horses made me brave.

After facing melanoma, I found my courage again by getting back on a horse. The horse trainer, Tom, called and said, "Heart is ready for you. I'm bringing her home."

"I'm not ready for her. They found cancer on my leg. It's been removed, but I can't walk yet. I don't know when I'll walk again."

"Then you'll need a good horse," Tom said. And he brought Heart home.

I was riding her before I could really walk again.

The plow had ripped five feet down into the soil, creating an impassable field on our farm. I rode along the edge of this destruction, my leg throbbing where the cancer had been removed. Heart was sniffing the ground, her nostrils flaring in alarm at the churned-up dirt bordering the trail we followed. She sensed the danger of a land torn asunder.

Horses are a flight animal. To run is their protection, but Heart couldn't do that here. Instinctively, she avoided the deep crevices of her once wide-open pasture of dry golden grass. The pasture that Soda Pop lived in before her. Waves of giant clods rolled like brown surf into the sunset. This was not a normally plowed field. The process of deep ripping was done by a Caterpillar D10 that had been shaking the ground for days. Overseeing this business of

Farming Grace

putting in our new orchard, Patrick said we were breaking the dirt as deep as we could to start anew.

It happened to coincide with a deep breaking in my life.

Heart and I hit the trail that skirted the plowed field. The way was narrow, ribboning between the furrowed ground and the steep ravine that borders our farm. We rode this path often. Change was coming but would take time. Our farm was in transition. Ten years from now, this orchard would be a beautiful ride for Heart and me. Even next spring would be nice, but today the field Soda Pop and I once galloped through with pure abandon was impossible for Heart.

She looked longingly at the far horizon but understood I couldn't take her there. Not with the field torn apart this way. She could break her leg in the deep plowing. A broken leg meant death for a horse. And just as I knew what Heart could and couldn't do, God knew me. He was the Farmer who had deeply plowed my life. I was just along for the ride.

Chapter Twenty-Four

> It always seems impossible until it's done.
> — Nelson Mandela

All the baby trees we planted in our new orchard were growing wild shoots. Hundreds of trees and thousands of tender shoots that had to be pruned away. I spent the day cutting the buds and shoots off the skinny little tree trunks. After each cut, I wiped my blade with disinfectant. I didn't want any bacteria getting into our young trees from the wounds I'd made on the trunks. We'd already designated the fruit-bearing branches we would keep on each little tree. Everything else had to come off. I'd never been so tired in my life. Not just because of farming, but I was working on two unfinished novels and also raising a houseful of children. I grew up with parents who taught me to never quit, so I wasn't leaving this orchard until the pruning job was done.

The labor was tedious. My hands cramped from all the cutting, and my back was tight and achy several hours into my labor. My jeans were covered in dirt. Pretty soon twenty-month-old Cruz found me and jumped onto my back in the orchard. I thought the work was hard until his sturdy little body joined mine.

Now his hands were locked around my neck, and he was laughing with joy. He loved his momma. I called for one of his older brothers to come get him. I still had rows of trees to prune. *Oh, Lord, help me. Give me strength to finish this job.* "Cruz, you have to get off my back. You're too heavy for Momma."

Cruz squeezed my neck harder. "I stay with you," he insisted.

A tear slid out of my eye. *Please give me strength, Lord.*

Ten-year-old John appeared down the row of trees. "He's done with us, Mom. He wants to be with you."

"Okay," I called back, wiping the tear from my cheek. "I'll watch him. Thank you, John."

"Sorry, Mom," red-haired John said in that earnest way of his. He was an old soul and such a good big brother. With the girls off at college, John had become my biggest help. I was so glad we named him John because my uncle John was gone. We'd buried him beside Uncle Dan, Grandma Helen, and Grandpa John when I was pregnant with Cruz.

How I missed my uncle John. He used to tell me I could marry more money in a minute than I could make in a lifetime.

"I will only marry for love," I always responded, and Uncle grinned and said, "Well, the sex better be damned good."

I smiled at my memories as I called to my son John, "It's all right. I can see the end of the orchard now. I should be done in another hour or two."

With Cruz on my back, it would take longer. My legs refused to lift me into a standing position. I finished the orchard on my knees with Cruz running around, jumping on and off my back. My toddler was so happy that I couldn't be frustrated with him. I was a mom first. A farmer second. A writer after that. Most of the time, I walked around with a story in my head. My husband called my characters my imaginary friends because when I told him about the books I was working on, I talked as if the characters were real people.

Stories fueled my life.

On my knees pruning the trees, I didn't realize I was in the middle of my own story and how it was about to get hard. Soon I would fall apart and look like all these little shoots on the ground scattered around me in the orchard.

Thank God I didn't know how badly I would break come spring.

Two weeks before leaving for that writers' conference at Mount Hermon, I stopped by the grocery store for some milk and to mail a package. In a hurry to get home to make supper, I noticed barbecue sauce on sale as I walked past the aisle in front of the deli. Grabbing a big, plastic bottle off the top shelf, I froze in my tracks when the sauce slipped through my fingers and exploded at my feet.

Sauce drenched me, coating my suede boots, my favorite Italian jeans, and my bright-pink sweater. Even speckling my face and dripping from my hair.

"Oh, no! I think your boots are ruined," said a twenty-something East Indian woman with a delightful British accent standing in front of the deli counter. The look of horror on her pretty face matched the feeling in my heart. The ladies working the deli stared at me aghast.

"I'm so sorry about the mess," I said.

I was longing to cry but sort of laughed. Weariness washed over me. My leg where I'd had the cancer removed throbbed like a jungle drum. I just wanted to go home, climb into bed, and cover my head. But I still held the package to mail in my hand, the samples of my writing bound for editors at Mount Hermon.

One of the deli ladies came out from behind the counter to help, but when she saw the sauce all over me and not much on the floor, she was speechless.

"I think I'll clean up in the bathroom," I told her. "I'll be back in a few minutes."

In the restroom I washed my face, amazed a plastic bottle could hit the floor and explode straight up like a volcano. After washing the sauce off my sweater, my shirtfront was soaked with water. So were my pants and boots after I scrubbed them the best I could. By then, I felt so humbled, it didn't matter that I had to walk through the store all wet.

I returned to the deli and apologized again for the mess, though by now the floor was clean and looked as if nothing had happened. A man stared at me, his eyes wide with questions. It wasn't raining outside, so I was sure he was trying to figure out why I was soaked.

Thank you, Lord, for humbling your servant, I prayed as I walked across the store to mail my package, then retrieved the milk and carried it to the checkout.

"What happened to you?" asked the lady working the cash register.

I told her about the sauce explosion, and she sympathetically checked out my boots.

"How bizarre," she said. "Your boots look terrible. What a bad day for you."

"They're just boots. It's okay."

I thanked the clerk for her compassion, which I deeply appreciated, and walked out of the store feeling like a whipped puppy.

Driving home, I realized I wasn't surprised about the sauce erupting on me. I was getting used to bad bounces. Again, I thanked God for humbling me. Had the sauce drenched me a few years back, my ruined boots would have done me in. But, on that day, the boots meant nothing. The money to buy them came from the Lord.

You give and take away… blessed be the name of the Lord (Job 1:21).

As I prayed, I reminded myself that no matter what happened, God was good.

God is good. God is good. God is good, I chanted, driving into the sunset with barbecue sauce in my hair. My leg hurt so much. I'd spent two months on the couch healing from the cancer surgery. The long tender scar on my calf reminded me that I was no longer who I used to be.

Cancer changes you.

I will restore you to health and heal your wounds whispered through my thoughts (Jeremiah 30:17). *For I know the plans I have for you. Plans to prosper and not harm you. Plans to give you a hope and a future* (Jeremiah 29:11). That was the first Bible verse I'd memorized after accepting Christ as my Savior. After facing melanoma, I felt like a brand-new believer all over again.

At home, Scott grinned when I described the sauce disaster at the grocery store.

"You're probably the topic of people's dinner conversation tonight." He laughed.

"I hope it makes people laugh. I wish I could laugh. I'm too tired for a sense of humor."

In the laundry room, I changed my clothes and sprayed cleaner on my sweater and jeans, then threw them in the washer. I began scrubbing my boots in our big steel sink beside the back door.

A few hours later after doing the dishes, bathing four squirming sons, and surviving the boys' homework blues, it was bedtime. I couldn't wait to test God on his promise: *"Because of the Lord's great love we are not consumed, for his compassions never fail. They are new every morning; great is your faithfulness"* (Lamentations 3:22–23).

I badly needed sleep and new mercies in the morning.

Early the next day as I dressed, with the birds singing outside my bedroom window, I heard the Holy Spirit say, *Stop feeling sorry for yourself.* The still, small voice shocked me almost as much as the sauce blowing up in my face the day before. The voice was gentle and loving but firm.

Tears streaked my cheeks. Cruz was yelling for me to come pour more milk into his sippy cup. Garry wanted his toast. I had already been up since five a.m. with Cruz and had gotten the older boys ready for school and out the door with their dad.

"I'm tired," I told the Holy Spirit as sobs shook my shoulders.

"Not one of all the Lord's good promises to the house of Israel failed; every one was fulfilled" (Joshua 21:45), the Holy Spirit impressed on my heart at that moment.

Over twenty years of raising toddlers—changing diapers and small, determined children dragging me out of bed, off the toilet, and away from my dream of becoming an author—I just felt tired standing there with the Holy Spirit convicting me of sin.

I knew self-pity had taken hold during my last pregnancy. Funny, the cancer on my leg started then too. At forty-three years old, while pregnant with Cruz, my friends were talking about hot flashes. My own personal brand of hot flashes consisted of me pregnant (again) and hollering at three little boys to obey me when they weren't obeying at all.

My friends were doing lunch, doing ministry, doing Pinterest.

I was pinning my jeans together, trying to avoid shopping for maternity clothes with moms half my age, while strapping diapers on our toddler, taking our five-year-old to speech class, doing homework with a seven-year-old, and dealing with three teenagers, too.

Now, after melanoma, I was fighting fear and self-pity, and struggling with being a tired mom with barbecue sauce in her hair.

I will restore you to health and heal your wounds. Trust in my promises. Trust in the Lord, whispered the Holy Spirit.

"All I have are your promises. I'm hanging on to my Bible like it's a lifeboat right now," I said to the Spirit.

The movie *The Life of Pi* flashed through my mind—that boy in the rowboat lost at sea with a tiger. I'd only seen parts of the movie because it disturbed me. But ten-year-old John really liked it, especially the tiger in the boat. He wanted me to watch it with him over and over again.

I felt as if God had put a tiger in my lifeboat.

That morning after the sauce mess, I realized the purpose of the tiger was to humble me. Also, to teach me once again to hold tight to the Word of God when no other source of rescue appeared on the horizon. When I didn't feel God's presence, didn't have God's peace, when the storm raged all around and the tiger was trying to eat me, the Bible was my only hope.

"Forgive me for feeling sorry for myself. Please heal me of self-pity and pride no matter how hard my life gets," I prayed that morning.

Two weeks later, my prayer was answered.

Chapter Twenty-Five

> They slipped briskly into an intimacy
> from which they never recovered.
> — F. Scott Fitzgerald

"Return to me," Scott said as he knelt beside my hospital bed.

I'd been sedated for several days after being handcuffed in our yard and taken away from the farm in an ambulance.

"Babe, come back," Scott insisted with so much pain and passion I snapped out of it for a moment and looked into his blue eyes filled with tears. So strange—my husband never cries.

I answered his tears with "Vaya con Dios." *Go with God,* though I don't speak Spanish. It was a line from one of my books.

Scott broke down, his big shoulders shaking with his sobs. My husband's grief confused me. I closed my eyes and went back to sleep.

Months later, Scott told me, "I thought that was it. The kids and I would be visiting you at the funny farm."

During that time, I lost all grip on reality. From the moment I collapsed in a Mount Hermon Writers Conference classroom on Monday morning, to waking up in the hospital on Thursday—the day before Good Friday—those days were a blur of darkness. The fact that I came home on Good Friday didn't escape me. I felt like I'd been in hell for three days.

While I was freaking out, Scott had let the neighbor boy come over. Jack was a fifth grader from across the field who played with our sons every day after school.

"I can't believe you didn't send Jack home," I told Scott once I was back in my right mind and home again. "Why did you let him see me that way?"

"Jack was the last thing on my mind. He's like one of our boys. I wasn't thinking about Jack when you were breaking sprinklers in the orchard with your bare hands."

"It's like people lost in the wilderness," the doctor kindly explained in her office during my checkup the following week. "Sometimes, when they're found, they are out of their minds. Dehydration and exposure can do this to a person."

"But I wasn't lost in the wilderness. I was at a Christian writers' conference," I told the doctor. She was sitting there with my hospital chart on her lap, all young and serious and set on making me healthy again.

"You were badly dehydrated. Your potassium was low. You're recovering from melanoma, and you keep having babies. You had an exhaustion breakdown," she insisted.

"But it felt like a spiritual breakdown," I replied.

None of the doctors wanted to deal with my spiritual questions. They maintained that my breakdown was purely physical. But I couldn't get past the spiritual. I felt so abandoned by God. Even betrayed by him. My breakdown began on Monday. But on Sunday, I sat in Mount Hermon's Palm Sunday service feeling so close to Jesus—as if he was breathing life and love into me that beautiful morning.

"I surrender everything to you," I told the Lord. "I am wholly and completely yours. I love you so much. I'll do anything for you."

What I heard back that morning in my spirit was this: *If you love me, feed my sheep.*

Why was I sensing, "*If you love me?*" Why was there an "if" in my love? Of course I loved Jesus.

Before dawn, that same Sunday morning, I walked down to the lounge and waited for someone to start the fire and bring out the coffee. That had become my morning routine at the conference, up very early to spend time with God in a warm place.

This particular morning, in the dark, a tall man in a stocking cap was walking to the lounge too. We struck up a conversation on the sidewalk together until, at the coffee cart, I realized he was a best-selling author and writing instructor at the conference. I was in a different mentoring class at Mount Hermon, so I was missing his talks that week. Now I was embarrassed. I'd never read his books, really didn't know who he was at all. But we were knee-deep in conversation by then, and I knew I was experiencing a God moment.

The author seemed to know this too. Either that or he was just being really nice because he sensed I was fragile. After we got our coffee, he sat me down by the fire in the lounge and gave me a blunt evaluation of why I wasn't published yet. He lasered in on my unwillingness to open up emotionally when I wrote. To write honestly. And bravely. And to hell with what people thought.

"Your next book, just let yourself go and write what's deep inside of you. Write it fast; don't stop and think about it."

What an amazing and wholly terrifying idea.

When I randomly bumped into him twelve hours later at the drugstore in town, both of us away from the conference grounds, we knew God was up to something.

"Life really isn't random this way," he said. "I want to send you one of my books. Please give me your address."

I gladly gave it to him.

After we talked, I picked up more Motrin for my aching leg, hurting so badly from walking all over Mount Hermon's hills. I had even stopped carrying water bottles in my bag and anything else in order to lighten my load. I could hardly sleep, partly from my throbbing leg and partly from spiritual unrest.

When my husband walked into the drugstore, I was happy to introduce him to the bestselling author. Scott had just arrived to drive me home on the following day.

After parting with the author and purchasing the Motrin, we headed back to Mount Hermon, where I tried to get some much-needed rest. But, again, I was up most of that night suffering leg pain and spiritual distress.

During the Monday morning worship, I finally fell apart. Painful memories surfaced out of nowhere. I couldn't stop crying. Returning to my room, I told Scott I was a mess.

"Let's just go home now," he suggested.

"I need to go to my mentoring class one last time. We aren't done with our critiques yet. The guys have been there for me. I want to be there for them."

Only two women were in the mentoring class—an older lady and me. Several of my classmates were pastors, and all were pleasant companions on the same writing journey.

The mentoring instructor had decided to lead us in a writing exercise. It felt meditative. The exercise focused on three events, but I can only recall two. The first is a blank in my memory. The second: Write down something that changed your life the summer of your sixteenth year. That was a time when my life got really confusing. I'd begun receiving obscene phone calls. Nothing terrible, just the same question asked over and over in a man's panting voice.

"Paula, what kind of panties do you have on?"

After a month of the phone calls, someone attempted to break into our house while I was home alone after school. My mom rushed back to the farm because she couldn't reach me by phone. The phone line had been cut with the molding stripped off the back door by someone trying to enter the house. My mom's car roared up the hill and must have scared the intruder away.

My mom called the police.

Investigators told her the farm was no longer a safe place for me after school. My parents moved me to a new high school in a different town and put me to work at my dad's engineering firm in the afternoon to keep an eye on me.

Before that confusing year ended, an older boy drove me home from a high school party. Though I'd flirted with this boy in the beginning, I thought he was cute, I'd made it clear to him that we were nothing more than friends. He said he was fine with only friendship, that he just wanted to drive me home.

It was no big deal, he said.

Instead, he drove me to an orchard and parked beside the trees. For a long time, this was my darkest wound. I was sexually assaulted in that orchard.

I fought back, so actual intercourse wasn't accomplished, but he was so strong and so worked up, he ejaculated on the back of my thighs before he could tear off my panties and penetrate me from behind. He had me pinned face down on the seat of his car. He then flipped me over and wiped semen from his hand inside my panties and into me as he restrained me.

"Oh, God, I tried to rape you," he confessed after that, sounding stunned and remorseful as he sprawled on top of me, begging for my forgiveness.

I was crying and refused to speak to him.

Finally, he gave up and let me go.

Battered and shocked, my clothes half torn off, I crawled out of that car into the mud on my hands and knees. The orchard had just been irrigated—the smell of wet dirt stayed with me for years.

As a teenager and into my twenties, I felt as if I had that scent on me. The smell of a watered orchard. A ripe aroma that made men want to defile me.

In college I was stalked by a student who ended up going to prison a few years later for raping girls. I was with Patrick when we ran into this student at a college bar before his arrest.

When this six-feet-something, two-hundred-pound guy wouldn't leave me alone, I slipped out the side door and ran away as my brother, all five feet six and a lean hundred and forty pounds of pure determination, got into a bar brawl with the guy. A bouncer ended up with stitches due to the stalker breaking a beer bottle and cutting people. He cut the bouncer's arm while trying to slice Patrick's throat.

After the bar brawl, the student rapist hated me. He found me alone at a gas station a few weeks later. When I locked myself in my car to escape him, he pressed his face to the driver's side window.

"I'll get you, b— ," he mouthed against the glass, leaving saliva on the windowpane.

A few days later, I was walking my dog through a quiet neighborhood, when this guy pulled up behind me in his car. My blood froze as he smiled at me. I ran through people's yards where he couldn't drive in order to escape him. How in the world had he found me miles away from the college?

Now, safe and sound at Mount Hermon, I sat there in class remembering all this, especially that sexual assault when I was seventeen. The clarity of it stunned me. I could smell the muddy orchard and taste the leather seat as that boy shoved me face down in his car.

There, with the instructor and my classmates, I couldn't write any of this down. It was so strange. I hadn't thought about these awful experiences in years, and the flood of memories traumatized me all over again.

In the last writing exercise, we were told to picture a scene in progress from our novel—a turning point in our story—as we were writing it. Then, envision an object in the story that hadn't been there before.

I was still trying to process the previous memories. How I cut my hair off and became bulimic in the wake of that sexual assault in high school. How I blamed myself for it happening. I shouldn't have drunk those two wine coolers at that party. Shouldn't have gone to those parties at all at my new high school, trying to fit in with the popular crowd. Shouldn't have trusted that older boy to take me home.

Only my best friend, Christy, knew what happened. She called the pregnancy hotline for me.

"Can you get pregnant if someone wipes semen on your privates with his hand?" Christy asked the nurse on the other end of the line.

Christy and I were virgins and weren't quite sure how things worked.

Now, I'm in that pivotal scene of my fictional story, the main character a teenage girl impregnated due to a rape she kept a secret from everyone.

I was attending the writer's conference with the hope that my literary agent could sell this particular novel, *The Mother Keeper,* to one of the publishers I had met there. In my scene, a shooting takes place. The main character's dad is drunk with a gun. There's a dog in the story, a beloved golden retriever, but he had never been part of my book until now. Duncan the golden retriever is the new object in the scene. This dog is mine, and I love him.

The drunk dad shoots Duncan.

I came unglued.

Not just in my mind, but in that classroom.

Chapter Twenty-Six

Courage, dear heart.

— C.S. Lewis

As I stood up from my seat, it felt as if a force from hell knocked me into some nearby chairs. I hit the ground, curled up in a ball, and remember only odd little clips of consciousness. Someone fetched my husband—it was only by the grace of God that Scott was there at Mount Hermon that morning. As I backed up in blind terror, Scott cornered me in the classroom along with one of the pastors, Lon, a humble man with a gentle spirit also taking the class.

Scott and Lon began to pray over me, and my sanity returned as they laid hands on me. Scott then led me from the room to his Dodge truck. I saw my classmates gathered around the instructor outside in the sunshine. They all looked so concerned. My grasp on reality was shaky at best, but I recall telling the group as I left that they were my brothers. I just don't know if I said it out loud or not.

Scott told me to wait in the truck while he collected our bags from our lodge room.

Driving home was mostly a blur, but I remember calling Kay.

"I don't know what happened," I told her. "I freaked out in my mentoring class at Mount Hermon."

Simultaneously, Scott was on his phone with a pastor from my class—not Lon but another pastor. He described to Scott how I used profanity after getting up off the floor. That I hit the teacher and called him a jackass when he tried to calm me down.

"You don't cuss," Scott said to me, baffled after he ended the call. "Did you really hit your writing mentor?"

"I don't know" is all I could say. The notion horrified me.

I had no memory of hitting anyone. No recollection after falling to the floor and tucking into a fetal position. It was only after Scott and Lon prayed over me that I came back to reality.

"Why would you call your teacher a jackass?" Scott asked, bewildered.

"We talked about horses and mules while getting coffee this morning. He laughed and called himself a jackass. It must have stuck in my head. I'm sure he's never had one of his students come sliding off the rails like this before."

All I could think was, *I'll never show my face at Mount Hermon again. My writing days are over.*

Next thing I knew, I was in our front yard having a total meltdown, ripping off my jeans and swearing.

"My wife was normal. She never cusses. She's a Christian." Scott tried to convince the sheriffs. But there I was, cussing like

Robert De Niro in *Scarface* with my jeans in shreds as they handcuffed me beside the ambulance. The first responders were convinced I'd taken drugs or been slipped drugs at Mount Hermon.

When they tested me for narcotics and a brain tumor at the hospital, they found nothing but dehydration, messed-up electrolytes, and low potassium. But a nurse at the hospital told me low potassium can kill you.

Hospital memories came in snapshots. I vaguely recall being placed in a tube, probably for the MRI, thinking the world was ending and this was a spaceship to get me off an exploding planet. Scott and my aunt Marolyn, a retired emergency room nurse, sat in nearby chairs, their heads bent in whispered conversation.

Why aren't they getting in the tube with me to get out of here?

A day or two later, I woke up in a hospital room and opened my eyes to Scott on his knees sobbing beside my bed. A day after that, I found Kay reading in a nearby chair. She appeared calm and peaceful in the morning light. I realized that I'd heard a man screaming in the night. A poor human soul confused and going crazy in a nearby room.

I had also heard nurses talking about my roommate—a woman on suicide watch. I don't know how I knew all this, but I did. These patients were mentally ill.

How did I end up here? I'd never suffered from depression, never considered suicide, never thought myself sick in the head, but I must have been sick because here I was.

No wonder my husband was crying.

Chapter Twenty-Seven

> The world breaks everyone, then some
> become strong at the broken places.
> — Ernest Hemingway, *A Farewell to Arms*

In the wake of my breakdown, I wondered if my Christian days were over along with my writing. Not my belief in Christ—God was bigger than ever in the light of my breakdown—but my belief in church. That I must be part of a religious community and lead a good churchgoing life. Wasn't that the mold I had just broken?

"God killed the church lady in me," I told Kay when she visited me at home. She downloaded *Daily Audio Bible* onto my iPad because I was too exhausted to read the Bible for myself.

I didn't think a real Christian could cuss like that, could lose it like that. Could slap my writing mentor. And my dad as he tried his best to calm me down in the yard before the ambulance hauled me away. I'd never hit anyone in my adult life, except halfheartedly spanking my children a few times. The spankings never worked; my sons only laughed at me, so I gave up with that wooden spoon that didn't hurt them because I couldn't bring myself to swing it hard enough.

Unbelievable.

I just couldn't fathom how this had happened to me.

After sleeping for several days with IVs pumping potassium, in my right mind again, I walked out of the hospital into Good Friday filled with hope.

It was as if I'd risen from the dead.

Easter was beautiful, but then reality hit on Monday, a week after leaving Mount Hermon. I was now the woman who freaked out at the conference. Emails from several classmates waited in my in-box, and I apologized as best I could to the other students and to my writing mentor for what happened. I tried to explain, repeating what the doctors said about an exhaustion breakdown, but the truth was, I didn't know what had really happened. It felt as if I had descended into hell there. As if demons dragged me kicking and screaming into some dark pit. When I thought about it, "crazy" came to mind. Maybe I was mentally ill. Maybe I needed some padded room therapy. But the Spirit in me resisted the notion.

"For I am convinced that neither death nor life, neither angels or demons, neither the present nor the future, nor any powers, neither height nor depth, nor anything else in all creation, will be able to separate us from the love of God that is in Christ Jesus our Lord" (Romans 8:38–39).

This Bible verse reassured me. I meditated on the promise that demons cannot separate me from God's love.

"I'm just glad you're a human being," a friend calling from out of town told me, having heard about the excitement. "I thought you were superwoman all these years."

We laughed and made small talk, but under the thread of conversation, I was a broken woman. Everybody knew it. I felt so fragile in church the following Sunday. Soon, I pulled out of all ministry. I was the last person who needed to help someone through a hard time. I kept blogging only because *"If you love me, feed my sheep"* was stuck in my head and in my heart. I now understood the "if" in the love that had escaped my understanding on Palm Sunday in Mount Hermon's chapel.

If you love me ...

It felt as if my faith had been stripped bare and burned through. But I still loved Jesus, so I blogged each week trying to make sense out of something I didn't understand. Maybe I will never fully and completely understand the breakdown I'd had. To my surprise, people who read the blog posts contacted me wanting to make sense out of things they didn't understand either.

In the wake of coming apart, I realized God had opened a new door for me to comfort people. They didn't care that I'd had a breakdown. Maybe it was because I'd had a breakdown that they wanted to talk to me. I now understood something many Christians didn't.

"God didn't do this to you. He didn't give you cancer and a breakdown. He doesn't do these kinds of things. God loves you," earnest Christian friends told me.

I heard this again and again following that vulnerable time. Then I sat alone reading the Book of Job. Before, I never liked the Book of Job in the Bible. Even avoided reading it. But now, the story of Job comforted me like nothing else could. Job knew God did that to him—by way of Satan—but still God said to Satan, "Have you considered my servant Job?"

Basically, God told Satan to rise up against Job to test Job's faith. When it was all said and done, Job cried out to God to end his suffering, and God said, *"Brace yourself like a man, I will question you and you will answer me, Job. Where were you when I laid the foundation of the earth? Tell me if you have understanding"* (Job 38:3–4).

I didn't have understanding. Neither did Job. God is bigger than human beings can understand. At the end of his story, Job said to God, *"My ears had heard of you, but now my eyes have seen you. Therefore, I despise myself and repent in dust and ashes"* (Job 42:5–6).

Job repented after God tested him.

Coming out of the hospital and seeing life in a different light, that was how I felt: God was bigger than I knew, and I repented of all that I was. Because when God reveals himself to you in a Job-like fashion, this is what happens. You fall on your face and realize church doesn't teach you this stuff. The evangelical church teaches God loves you. That he'll never hurt you. But you can find the exact opposite in your Bible. Sometimes God wounds, but he also heals (Job 5:18).

A week after I came home from the hospital, our neighbor boy, Jack, came over. My sons weren't home from school yet. But Jack, blond and cute as apple pie, stood at the front door with an expectant smile on his face. I could tell he wanted to wait with me for the boys the way he always did—sitting happily on our couch watching a movie with two-year-old Cruz. But all I could think of was why would Jack want to hang out with a crazy lady?

There I was, peering through the slit in the door, afraid to let him in. Not only into the house but into my post-breakdown world.

"I'm sorry I freaked out like that before Easter when you were here," I started tentatively.

I didn't remember Jack in the yard before the ambulance came, but I was sure *he* remembered it.

Jack grinned. "That's okay," he said, like it didn't matter at all.

I could tell he really wanted to come into the house, so I stepped aside, my mind whirling with what else I should say. *Do I explain to this eleven-year-old what a mental collapse is? Maybe his dad has already explained it to him.* I stopped my mind from imagining what Jack's dad had told him and what other people were saying about me.

But Jack was the same old Jack.

He walked over to the couch and made himself comfortable beside a sleepy Cruz, who was up from his nap watching a movie. The two looked so precious sitting there together lost in *A Bug's Life*.

I walked down the hall to my bedroom and found myself sobbing into my hands. This little boy didn't care that I was just out of a mental ward. He wanted to be here with me. He was growing up with a single dad. He needed me, and I needed him at that point in our lives. The grace that came through that child stunned me.

When my sons got home, I made the boys an early dinner of mac and cheese. Jack was laughing at the kitchen bar counter with

John, Joey, Garry, and Cruz. Nothing had changed with these five boys. They expected hugs and food and cleanup from me just as it had always been.

Their confidence in me felt so undeserved ... but I took it just the same.

For years, I'd lived too tired, too scared, too twisted tight. Wrapped round and round until I came unwound. Some women dream of tearing their clothes and screaming, "I'm done with this s—t!" I had done that. My favorite Italian jeans destroyed. My sweatshirt stained with blood from my wounded hands. I'd broken sprinklers off in the orchard, kicking them, and pulling on them, cutting my hands in the process.

The shame came in waves, washing me to the cross where Jesus bore all my shame. How does a broken woman make it all go away as she makes dinner? Makes beds? Makes Easter memories for her children?

My second day home from the hospital after my breakdown, we colored eggs, went on the church Easter egg hunt, and watched *It's the Easter Beagle, Charlie Brown.*

So many questions I felt too fragile to answer.

I'd snapped.

I was sorry, but people fail.

All the time humans fail. We fail each other. We fail ourselves. Most of all, we fail Christ. But his grace was enough. And my husband had big shoulders. I'd married him for that. All my life I'd looked for a man to protect me. Knowing I was weak. Knowing men were strong. Knowing it could go either way. Before Jesus, I'd searched men's eyes for sin or salvation.

Men had taken care of me, and men had abused me. Before I came to the Lord, I put my hope in men.

"God did something in all of us through your breakdown," Scott told me one morning as we sat in our living room chairs beside the fireplace, drinking coffee out of fine-boned china cups covered in pink roses. I loved that my husband with the big shoulders and football scar on his lip loved rose-covered china the way I did.

"I'm not who I used to be," I told Scott, holding my coffee cup up to my lips, blowing gently before I took a sip. The morning sun slanted through our windows, filling our home with golden light.

"None of us are." Scott looked into my eyes and smiled. "God has changed us."

The china cups in our hands were so delicate. It was a wonder the flowery vessels survived our farm and our boys. They also survived the microwave, dishwasher, and our burning coffee. And it hit me—the fragile porcelain survived fire because it had been tested by fire.

So had we.

And I leaned hard on the man I married who didn't hold my breakdown against me but held me against his chest. We'd been through so much. I was weaker, but we were stronger for it. Our love had withstood my breaking.

My little green John Deere tractor fits me just right. I cut our lawn and then mowed the orchard, driving carefully around our blooming peach trees with bees buzzing in the flowers.

Mowing soothed me.

Being out in the sunshine on a perfect spring day doing farm work brought me peace. In a few months, I'd be selling our family's cherries, apricots, pluots, nectarines, and peaches at the farmers' markets. Until now, I'd avoided farming because I was set on being a writer, not a farmer, but the medical bills were pouring in from my cancer and the hospital stay from my breakdown. Insurance had all but failed us. By the end of the summer, we were dead broke and farming in earnest with my family.

Scott picked the fruit with Oma—my mom in her seventies. My brother Patrick and son-in-law Drew took care of the trees. Dad drove the tractor. I sold the fruit, and our boys, the ones old enough to work, labored alongside us.

I thought about my great-grandma Delcie Mae, the girl who walked to California beside a covered wagon because of a no-good man. Her mother, Elizabeth, my hero, the woman who shook her fist at men on the river, took a job in Sanger, California, becoming the housekeeper of the widowed farmer, Mike Phillips.

Elizabeth married Mike, and a handful of years later, Delcie Mae married Mike's son, Albert. Delcie and Albert went from being stepbrother and stepsister to husband and wife. Together, they moved to Yuba City, California, where they planted a peach orchard. When she was old, Dell, as most folks called her, kept a Bible on her lap and sang hymns to anyone who would listen. Her son Jack became a peach farmer too. Jack's daughter, Carolyn, my mom, Oma, oversees the farming business my family returned to a few years back. Then there is me, a fifth-generation California farmer now, thanks to a well-timed breakdown.

The dirt, sunshine, and old-fashioned pace of farming agreed with me. I found myself healing the same way we grew our fruit: slowly, day by day, and dependent on God. Every farmer looks to the sky, waiting on the weather. Waiting on God's providence. California was in a drought as we planted our new orchards, expanding our farming business while hoping for rain.

Our wells were deep and good, but there was talk of the state taking control of the water, even cutting off farmers to send water to Southern California's thirsty cities. I left the water in God's hands.

The wells were his, and I am his.

And when people questioned why we were planting new orchards in a drought-parched land, I told them we were trusting God and farming on grace.

Epilogue

> Live in each season as it passes; breathe
> the air, drink the drink, taste the fruit,
> and resign yourself to the influence of each.
> — Henry David Thoreau

I never meant to write a memoir. Fiction is my sweet spot. I love making up stories, but after my breakdown, I could no longer ignore the pull to put into words our family's redemption. How we returned to God and the farm together. I am grateful God made me a writer, but even more grateful he has returned me to farming. There is something about our farm that is so good for my body. For my mind. For my soul.

The Bible says the sleep of a laborer is sweet. And it is. During harvest season I sleep like our growing boys, hard and heavy and good. So good. Before becoming a farmer, sleep was a battle for me. During the winter months when I'm writing, I return to this battle. My brain won't shut off when I go to bed. It reminds me of a little hamster I used to have that would go mad on her wheel. This is what my mind feels like during writing season, running in circles, the endless pounding of ideas and memories and characters talking in my head. Sometimes my little hamster would run so fast she would flip herself off her wheel and lie there shocked at herself in her cage.

My breakdown flipped me off my wheel. I was shocked at myself. I was afraid I'd never be the same. And thank goodness I'm not the same.

I am better after breaking.

I needed to break to learn to live on grace.

All my life I've longed to be a strong woman. I never found true strength in myself. Instead, I found the strength I so longed for in Jesus.

The day I came home from the hospital, I went out and got on my little John Deere tractor and mowed our orchard. The peaches were in bloom and looked so beautiful in the afternoon light. While I rode on that tractor, God's grace found me and freed me, and I knew with all my heart I'd finally come home to the farm for good.

Two months later I was selling our family's fruit at the farmers' markets and tending my large country garden. There's nothing like a homegrown tomato. And along with farming the land, I found myself farming grace.

I don't believe you can earn grace, but I believe you can farm it. You can plant grace and tend grace and harvest grace in your life. You can feed your family grace and feed yourself grace and feed this big, bad, beautiful world grace.

But first, you must acquire the seeds of grace. Seeds that come from only one source—the original Farmer. The God of amazing grace.

The drought is over. As I write this epilogue, California looks like the Garden of Eden, so lush and green and covered in wildflowers. Our orchards are in bloom. They smell so sweet and look so stunning. I wish you were here to take a walk in the orchard with me. I would tell you I never thought anything good could come out of that night I was sexually assaulted in that orchard. But this past summer, out of the blue and out of the vendors' booths woven together like a tapestry at the farmers' market, came a man who called my name. I was in the middle of selling peaches and pluots on this warm July morning with the sun on my face. I looked up, locking eyes with the man. I had no idea who he was, though something in my spirit paused and took a deep breath.

"You don't know me," the man said, and I heard his disappointment.

He looked old and tired, kind of overweight, but I didn't recognize him, though that check in my spirit expanded. I happened to be standing outside of our booth because I'd just been talking to a customer, a young mom in a baseball cap.

Then the man approaching me said his name, stepped closer, and reached out as if I was his long-lost friend. Before he hugged me tightly, in his eyes, I saw that boy who drove me to a muddy orchard, sexually assaulted me, then drove me home with torn, mud-smeared clothes and a shattered spirit.

I whispered a silent prayer. *God, help me respond with your mercy and lovingkindness, though this man doesn't deserve it. Help me love my enemy. Oh, Jesus, help me....*

I let him hug me, this person who once hurt me so deeply. And at the end of that embrace I took another deep breath and stepped back from him.

He rolled into small talk—all the things you say when you haven't seen a person in three decades—as I stood there smiling, nodding my head, and responding politely. Reminding myself that Christ loved his enemies and I could too because Jesus was in me.

I inhaled deeply, hoping to suck in the Spirit of God. The strength of God. The mercy of God.

Scott, bagging up fruit for customers on the other side of our stand, flexed his muscles in our direction, letting me know he saw us. He must have sensed my distress. My husband reads me so well. And as I stood with this boy from my past, now a middle-aged man with a weary countenance—this man I would never have recognized without his calling my name—I thanked God for my handsome husband who keeps me safe.

"I drove your wife home from a party one night," the man laughingly told Scott when he stepped over between serving customers. Scott nodded and looked at me like, *Are you okay with this guy?* My gaze told him I was okay. After all these years of marriage, we can carry on a conversation with just our eyes, which comes in handy at times like these.

After checking on me, Scott returned to our customers. That's when something in my spirit clicked, like the safety clicking off on a gun. This man wasn't sorry for assaulting me when I was seventeen. He stood there looking at me like the cat that ate the canary.

"You look so good, so happy. What's your secret?" The man checked me out from head to toe, his gaze all too knowing.

"I accepted Christ as my Savior, and this has made me happy."

He stood there looking bemused. The way people look when you've said something that astounds them. I talked about Jesus for a while, the man nodded, his smile disappearing, his gaze growing distant, and then he walked away.

I didn't know I would feel good when he left, but I did. I'd given grace and forgiveness when it wasn't deserved. Before my breakdown, when they handcuffed me in our front yard and tucked me into an ambulance, and before facing this boy—now a man at the farmers' market more than a quarter of a century after he sexually assaulted me—I believed you earned everything you got. But I've learned grace can't be earned.

Grace is like the gift of a good crop.

We work really hard in the orchard, but God gives us the harvest. God sends the rain. The sunshine. The bees. Did you know without bees the world would end? There is a process of reaping and sowing but miracles too when it comes to grace.

Just like what happens in our orchard. In the plowing. In the pruning. In the light shining down from the sun. In the sweet, clean water rising up from our deep well that irrigates our orchards through little sprinklers at the base of each tree. Humans are like trees. We depend on God for light, water, plowing and pruning, the fruit we bear in our lives. And we need bees. We must be pollinated by grace. We may not know it, but we live on God's collective grace here on earth.

The Bible says fear of the Lord is the beginning of wisdom (Proverbs 9:10). Just the beginning. There's so much more to learn. Because there is no fear in love. God's perfect love casts out fear (1 John 4:18).

Growing up on the farm with the tough cowboy dad I had, I learned to handle a lot. My dad never allowed giving up. You did what you had to do. You got the job done. And you didn't cry about it. If you were upset, you went out and rode your pony hard.

This is what many of us are doing. We are riding our horses hard. But living this way will eventually wear you out. It will bring you to the end of yourself.

At least I hope it brings you to the end of yourself.

Because that's where grace blooms.

During harvest season, Scott and I do date nights in the orchard. We've made this promise to ourselves, to our marriage, even during harvest season: Friday nights belong to us. It amazes me we still have the energy to romance each other after we've picked, packed, and delivered to Raley's and Bel Air supermarkets already that day. Then we pick another load of fruit, since we leave before dawn on Saturday mornings for the farmers' market. I pour wine into tin cups, and we do a pick and sip in the orchard. Kind of like a paint and sip where you go and drink wine and paint pictures at some art studio with a little bar in the back.

I've only gone to one paint and sip, and I laughed a lot. The women there thought they were painting really well. I thought they were drinking really well. I ended up not having any wine because five minutes into painting, I realized there was no way I could drink *and* paint, especially when the ladies beside me began comparing the poppies they were painting to a man's privates. They would not stop laughing about it.

The instructor, a surprisingly serious woman, told everyone to pay attention and create good art. She reminded me of a drill sergeant as the bartender walked over to refill the laughing ladies' wine glasses. They kept talking about man parts like farmers talk about fruit and nuts. I gave my daughter Cami, painting beside me, big eyes, like can you believe what these women are saying?

Cami smiled her sweet smile and kept on painting.

In the end my poppies actually looked like flowers, but the ladies beside me painted flowers that looked like bananas. The instructor frowned at their drunken elongated flowers, but when she looked at my canvas, she said, "Your middle poppy is really good."

Her praise delighted me. We'd all painted three poppies. I liked my middle flower best too. It looked as if a real artist had painted that poppy. Sometimes this happens. Sometimes I surprise myself.

In the orchard with my husband, I'm surprised by how much we enjoy our date nights. We stop and kiss, our mouths tasting like wine, both of us sweaty from all our picking. I find our love in the orchard a miracle. There's usually a soft breeze in the evenings on our farm, especially during early summer. The June nights are so pleasant, the smell of ripening fruit intoxicating. The setting sun feels heavy but good, like my husband's embrace. Scott has powerful muscles, and when he wraps his arms around me, his strength is irresistible. We're both wearing picking buckets, so there are always double buckets between us we must overcome to kiss.

"Let's bump buckets," Scott says after kissing, and I giggle like a teenager.

I know. It's sappy, and yet it's all I've ever wanted. To fall in love in an orchard again and again. The devil tried to take this from me, but God has restored it a hundredfold. And he can restore your life too. I dare you to just give the Lord your heart and soul and see what happens.

THE END

Acknowledgments

I didn't write this story to reveal our family secrets. I wrote it to share our family's redemption. I've changed the names and appearances of some individuals in this story and in a few instances modified settings to preserve anonymity.

To my dream team of editors: Kimberly Shumate, Susanne Lakin, Alice Crider, Janet McHenry, and Judy Gordon Morrow, you ladies are wise and tender midwives helping give birth to this book. To my precious critique partners, Michelle Shocklee and Katherine Scott Jones, thank you for over a decade of love and edits. Thank you to our neighbors, Reece and Teresa Cordi of Cordi Winery, for the use of their Sutter Buttes image. I also want to thank Karen Ball for encouraging me to write this memoir in the first place, and Alice Crider for being a magnificent author coach.

Cami and Kay, thank you so much for reading it more times than you probably wanted to while helping me fix mistakes. And Lacy, who made it through nursing school while I worked on this story and often sent me Pinterest pins that said, "You can do it!

Keep going! Don't quit!" I'm so grateful neither of us gave up on dreams. And to our sons: Luke, John, Joseph, Garry, and Christian, you boys make me laugh and catch my breath when you scare and delight me every day.

To my mom and dad, Oma and Opa, for being willing to let me share their story too. In their golden years, their marriage is sweet now. And thanks to my big brother Patrick, who has always been my first protector.

To my forever protector, Scott, our great romance has surprised and astonished me. You're my soulmate, Babe. I will always love you.

Most of all, I want to thank Jesus for his redeeming love, and you, dear reader. Writing this story helped me to heal. I hope somehow you find some healing in it for your own life too. I'm praying for you.

Love,
Paula

Made in the USA
San Bernardino, CA
13 November 2019

59865961R00156